MISSIOLOGICAL
IMPLICATIONS
OF
EPISTEMOLOGICAL
SHIFTS

Christian Mission and Modern Culture

EDITED BY
ALAN NEELY, H. WAYNE PIPKIN,
AND WILBERT R. SHENK

In the Series:

Into the Vacuum,
by Gordon Scoville

Speaking the Truth in Love,
by James V. Brownson

From Complicity to Encounter,
by Jane Collier and Rafael Esteban

Canon and Mission,
by H. D. Beeby

*Missiological Implications of
Epistemological Shifts,*
by Paul G. Hiebert

Trinity Press International, P.O. Box 1321, Harrisburg, PA 17105

Trinity Press International is a division of The Morehouse Group.

Scripture quotations are from the Revised Standard Version Bible, copyright 1973, Division of Christian Education of the National Council of the Churches of Christ in the United States of America, and are used by permission.

Cover design: Brian Preuss

Library of Congress Cataloging-in-Publication Data

Hiebert, Paul G., 1932–
    The missiological implications of epistemological shifts : affirming truth in a modern world / Paul G. Hiebert.
        p. cm. — (Christian mission and modern culture)
      Includes bibliographical references.
      ISBN 1-56338-259-8 (pbk. : alk. paper)
      1. Missions—Theory. 2. Philosophy and religion.
3. Knowledge, Theory of (Religion). 4. Critical realism.
I. Title. II. Series.
    BV2063.H464   1998
    266'.001—dc21   98–48832
                                       CIP

Printed in the United States of America
99 00 01 02 03 04 6 5 4 3 2 1

MISSIOLOGICAL IMPLICATIONS

OF

EPISTEMOLOGICAL SHIFTS

AFFIRMING TRUTH IN A MODERN/POSTMODERN WORLD

PAUL G. HIEBERT

TRINITY PRESS
INTERNATIONAL
HARRISBURG, PENNSYLVANIA

Contents

96396

List of Figures

Preface to the Series

Both Christian mission and modern culture, widely regarded as antagonists, are in crisis. The emergence of the modern mission movement in the early nineteenth century cannot be understood apart from the rise of technocratic society. Now, at the end of the twentieth century, both modern culture and Christian mission face an uncertain future.

One of the developments integral to modernity was the way the role of religion in culture was redefined. Whereas religion had played an authoritative role in the culture of Christendom, modern culture was highly critical of religion and increasingly secular in its assumptions. A sustained effort was made to banish religion to the backwaters of modern culture.

The decade of the 1980s witnessed further momentous developments on the geopolitical front with the collapse of communism. In the aftermath of the breakup of the system of power blocs that dominated international relations for a generation, it is clear that religion has survived even if its institutionalization has undergone deep change and its future forms are unclear. Secularism continues to oppose religion, while technology has emerged as a major source of power and authority in modern culture. Both confront Christian faith with fundamental questions.

The purpose of this series is to probe these developments from a variety of angles with a view to helping the church understand its missional responsibility to a culture in crisis. One important resource is the church's experience of two centuries of cross-cultural mission that has reshaped the church into a global Christian *ecumene*. The focus of our inquiry will be the church in modern culture. The series (1) examines modern/postmodern culture from a missional point of view; (2) develops the theological agenda that the church in modern culture must address in order to recover its own integrity; and (3) tests fresh conceptualizations of the nature and mission of the church as it engages modern culture. In other words, these volumes are intended to be a forum where conventional assumptions can be challenged and alternative formulations explored.

This series is a project authorized by the Institute of Mennonite Studies, research agency of the Associated Mennonite Biblical Seminary, and supported by a generous grant from the Pew Charitable Trusts.

Introduction

It is presumptuous of me, I know, to write on the epistemological shifts now taking place in Western cultures. I have had little formal training in philosophy, and the topic is far too broad for a brief treatment such as this. But my work in missions and anthropology made it impossible for me to avoid the question of epistemology and its impact on how we view and do missions.

My interest in the subject springs from two lifelong concerns. The first has to do with my commitment to Christian missions. Growing up in a mission setting in India and having Indian friends, I was aware of the need (a) to understand cultures in order to communicate and contextualize the gospel in different settings with a minimum of distortion and (b) to know social systems in order to encourage the development of vital indigenous churches. This concern was a major reason for my studying anthropology.

During my years as a missionary in India, I increasingly felt the need to examine the Western cultural biases of American missions and how these shaped the way we understood Scripture, theology, the nature of the missionary task, and our response to non-Christian religions. I also realized that the Scriptures themselves were given in cultural and historical contexts, and that I needed to understand these if I wanted to understand the Scriptures better.

Intercultural ministries raise many critical questions we can ignore (to our peril) so long as we live and work only with people of "our own kind." For example, what must a new convert know or believe in order to be saved? Can a person who hears the gospel for the first time at a street meeting or on the radio be truly converted? How can we translate and communicate the Scriptures interculturally without distorting their message? And what is the relationship of the gospel to human cultural, social, and historical contexts; of missionaries to the people they serve; of Christian believers to their nonbelieving neighbors; of the church as the divine body of Christ to churches as human organizations; and of the divine nature of Christ to his full humanity as Jesus? Why do we demand radical changes and great sacrifices of new converts when in our homelands Christianity is largely captive to our cultural and social systems? How should we do missions in an anticolonial, postmodern era characterized by religious relativism and accusations of Christian imperialism? Struggling with these questions, I became aware of the epistemological foundations that underlay them and experienced a shift from a theology and anthropology based on positivism to ones based on critical realism. The change affected the way I viewed my ministry, my relationship to my Indian colleagues, and my witness to non-Christians.

My second concern was the integration of theology and anthropology in the task of missions. I am a committed evangelical Anabaptist who takes both Scriptures and theology seriously. I am also an anthropologist committed to an understanding of humans and their historical and sociocultural contexts. The integration of these two disciplines was not easy. I was taught that theology is rooted in beliefs and science in facts, but I was uneasy about this solution. I learned that theology deals with ultimate spiritual concerns and science with this-worldly matters, but this juxtaposition did not fit the teachings in the Bible. If I judged theology using the evidential criteria of science, theology fell short. If I judged anthropology in the light of theology, anthropology was woefully inadequate to deal with the real story of human existence.

The picture changed as anthropologists began to see that science, including anthropology, is rooted in a modern worldview and is as much based on a belief in fundamental presuppositions as is theology. The two are not different ways of knowing but are systems of knowledge seeking to answer different but related questions. This awareness of the cultural and subjective nature of knowledge made it easier to integrate theology and science, but it raised even more difficult questions of cognitive and moral relativism. The cure was worse than the disease. By the 1970s most anthropologists had abandoned radical cultural relativism because of the nihilism implicit in it.

It was clear to me that I needed a new epistemological foundation on which to base both my theology and my anthropology. It was clear that I could not bring the two together if they were built on different epistemologies. It was then that I discovered the critical approach to realism advocated by Charles Peirce, Ian Barbour, and others. This avoided the arrogance and colonialism implicit in positivism and the relativism of instrumentalism. I found that it fit closely with the teachings of Jesus, Paul, and the other New Testament writers. It also made theology a living reality in my life, touching every area of my thought life. This volume reflects my own pilgrimage in seeking to integrate theology and anthropology in the cause of missions and in discovering my evangelical Anabaptist roots.

1

The Epistemological Foundations of Positivism

The West today is navigating a sea change that threatens to capsize it. On the surface, cross-waves of debate occur between technological advance and ecological preservation, between the claims of science and the affirmation of other cultures, and between the uniqueness of Christianity and the recognition of other religions. Below the surface, the deep currents of traditionalism, modernity, and postmodernity; of globalism and ethnic particularism; and of truth and relativism collide in different ways in different lands. As Christian theologians and missionaries, we seek to be rooted in biblical thought, but we live in human contexts that profoundly shape our thoughts.[1] It should not surprise us that we are influenced by these currents around us.

Underlying this sea change is a clash of epistemologies. The cognitive assumptions of modernity on which the West was built are being challenged by postmodernism on the one hand and by the revival of traditionalism and fundamentalism on the other. To give a biblical critique and response in these confusing times, it is important that we understand the epistemologies that underlie these various movements and our own theologies.

Positivism and Modern Science

The modern era began with the rise of ontological realism.[2] As Herbert Butterfield (1950) and others have pointed out,

1

Christianity provided the foundations on which the modern sciences were built. Basic to science is the assumption that there is a real world characterized by an intrinsic order that continues through time, and that human minds can, in some way, rationally comprehend this order through experience. This realism was foundational to the Hebraic worldview found in the Bible.

During the Middle Ages, however, this Hebraic worldview was replaced by theologies modeled along the lines of Greek philosophy. In its confrontation with Greek thought, the church adopted Greek philosophical weapons and used them against the pagan philosophers. In the process, however, the Hebrew worldview, which found meaning in history and story, was replaced by the Greek interests in the ultimate, unchanging structures of reality. Plato's dualism was widely accepted in academic circles. It divided reality into two realms: (1) the material realm, which was held to be an imperfect, transitory shadow of (2) the spiritual realm, which was seen as permanent, unchanging, and perfect ideal forms. For Christian scholars, the latter was seen as more important, the only reality worthy of the theologian's time. Augustine, who was profoundly interested in empirical knowledge before his conversion, wrote: "Nor dost Thou draw near but to the contrite in heart, nor art Thou? found by the proud, no, not though by curious skill they could number the stars and sand, and measure the starry heavens, and track the course of planets" (1976:91).

Platonism not only played an important role in the philosophical and theological divorce that separated ultimate concerns from matters of this world and emphasized the former to the neglect of the latter; it also provided the roots for the secularism that characterizes much of contemporary scientific thought. It replaced the fundamental Hebraic contingent dualism of "Creator" and "Creation" with an eternal dualism of "Supernatural" and "Natural." This division, which assumes an autonomous material world that can be explained fully in natural terms, restricts God's activities to the supernatural realm. The Renaissance turned Platonic idealism on its head by affirming the importance of the material over the spiritual world.

Key to the emergence of modern science was the rise of a logical empiricist, or "positivist," approach to knowledge. The terms *positivisme* and *positiviste* were coined by Auguste Comte. He argued for a new kind of certain knowledge based on the following principles: introspection must be rejected, and the empirical methods of the natural sciences that seek simply to describe sensory experiences must be adopted as the only acceptable scientific method; and the purpose of science is to formulate universal and immutable laws that must be verified by the facts of experience. Implicit in his method was a dichotomy between concept and reality, and between subject and known object. Later the terms "positivism" and "postpositivism" came to be used for what some call logical empiricism, a form of empiricism that views knowledge as a passive copy of reality. Today positivism is widely used as a label for the general epistemological foundations underlying much of modern scientific thought (cf. Laudin 1996; Fuller 1991; Leplin 1984).[3]

For the most part, hard scientists are not philosophers and do not bother themselves unduly with questions of epistemology. They have gone their way independent of philosophy because they are no more interested than are historians in the problems of skepticism, existence, and ultimate reality. They assume the reality of the material world—the primordial givenness of the facts that confront them—and the ability of their minds to perceive and understand this reality. Until recently they have refused to allow epistemological questions to obstruct their studies. Edmund Husserl calls this the "dogmatic standpoint" of the sciences. It is particularly in the social sciences and the philosophy of science that questions about the epistemological foundations of modern science are being raised.

Characteristics of Positivism

Confident in the validity of the scientific method, which to them seems self-evident in view of the results, most scientists have shown little interest in the mental processes by means of which they come to their conclusions despite numerous attempts to discredit them (Laudin 1996:149). They operate in the context of uncritical or naive realism, sometimes labeled positivism. Ian Barbour points out (1974:3–4) that "with a few exceptions, most scientists until the present century assumed that scientific theories were accurate descriptions of the world as it is in itself." This stance seemed justified in view of the great strides made by science in the acquisition of knowledge, particularly when compared with the apparent wanderings of medieval philosophy. Implicit in this uncritical stance are several assumptions that we need to examine.

Objective Realism

The first assumption of positivism is an ontological one, namely, that there is a real world outside our minds—one that exists apart from our knowledge of it. As Kathleen Nott observes:

> For most of us there "is" an "external" world, and however much we may affect it or interact with it by our explorations,... we think of it not only as somehow existing in its own right but also that its "real" description is somehow exhausted by the categories and calculations of physical science (1971:157–58).

In philosophy this assumption led to debates over the nature of *realis* and *realitas*. These words were invented by philosophers in the thirteenth century, and their meanings were assumed to be perfectly clear and obvious. Something is *real* if it has such and such characteristics, whether or not anyone thinks it has them. In other words, a Real is anything not affected by human cognitions *about it.*

The contrast between philosophical idealism and scientific realism can be seen in scientists' response to this term. From the outset, scientists assumed a real world and began to explore it by systematically examining those primordial or brute sense experiences that cannot be reduced to anything else or shown to be illusions. They explored that which

insists on forcing its way into human recognition as something other than the mind's creation. Upon this seemingly
hard reality they sought to build their knowledge.
Philosophical idealists, on the other hand, saw reality as
largely a creation of the human mind and sought by means
of reason to explicate the meaning of *ding an sich* (the thing
in itself). As Charles Peirce sees it, this task was doomed
from the start.

> In half a dozen ways the *Ding an sich* has been proved
> to be nonsensical.... [It] can neither be indicated or
> found. Consequently, no propositions can refer to it,
> and nothing true or false can be predicted of it.
> Therefore, all references to it must be thrown out as
> meaningless surplusage. But when that is done, we see
> clearly that Kant regards Space, Time and his
> Categories just as everyone else does, and never
> doubts or has doubted their objectivity (1955:299).[4]

The method par excellence by which scientists sought to
examine the real world was to begin with skepticism regarding all knowledge and to apply reason to systematic empirical
observations. In this the experimenter formulated a hypothesis about the nature of some reality based on earlier observations. The hypothesis in itself reflected a measure of sincere
doubt, for if the scientists had no doubt, further experimentation was unnecessary. The next step was to conduct experiments or observations to test the hypothesis. The hypothesis
was accepted or rejected on the basis of repeated empirical
tests. If it was confirmed, it became a "fact" like other facts.

This naturalistic view works well in the physical sciences,
but it faces a problem in studying humans. Either it must
reduce them to material objects, like other objects, or it
must admit their subjectivity and, therefore, an inability to
truly know them. There is little room for intersubjective
human communication or for people to reveal their inner
beliefs and feelings.

The extreme forms of this empiricism, sometimes
referred to as scientism, led to a denial of metaphysics and

of knowledge that does not ultimately rest on a form of empirical sense perceptions that can be repeated and verified independently. The result was a separation of science from its theological and philosophical rivals, and a growing agnosticism that denied transempirical realities.[5] Naturalistic forms of positivism are intrinsically secular in nature. Ernest Gellner writes:

> [In positivism] there are no privileged or a priori *substantive* truths. (This, at one fell swoop, eliminates the sacred from the world.) All facts and all observers are equal. There are no privileged Sources or Affirmations, and all of them can be queried (1992:80).

In other words, the materialistic forms of positivism deny religious transcendence and revelation, and affirm that everything is found in a single, orderly system of nature, the most fundamental realities of which are bits of material substance.

Modern scientific materialism is based on a mechanistic view of nature.[6] The physical world was seen as a perfect machine that could be controlled by those who had full knowledge of how it worked. Even the human being came to be seen as "man-the-machine." The parts act on one another in predetermined ways that are governed by impersonal, unchanging laws or principles that determine the one possible outcome for each event. It is these laws, not mere facts, that are universal. They state that *whenever* certain conditions are met (including those in the future) certain results will occur. For example, when scientists speak of "the law of gravity" they do not mean any particular event that has happened in the past, but what surely happens, past or future, to everything that fulfills certain conditions. The result is a linear view of causality.

This mechanical view of causation obviously leaves no place for purpose or teleology. It focuses on the primary causes of an event—questions of *how*, and ignores secondary causes—questions of *why*. This has enabled scientists to predict and to control many areas of nature. But as Harold Schilling points out, according to this view the world is "closed, essentially completed and unchanging, basically substantive, simple and shallow, and fundamentally unmysterious—a rigidly programmed machine" (1973:44). Furthermore, in their study of humans, positivists have little need of dealing with questions of hermeneutics or of trying to understand what is in their minds.

Positivism is an attempt to acquire certain, objective knowledge about the material world. Immanuel Wallerstein notes:

The natural sciences were epistemologically very stable from about the 16th or 17th century to the 1970s, in the sense that Newtonian/Cartesian premises were fundamental to all scientific activity. Science was the search for the simplest laws. Science was objective. Science was neutral. Science dealt with equilibria. Science was cumulative (1996:5).

Positivists set out to construct science on fully objective, or "positive," knowledge—a new kind of objective empirical knowledge not found in previous history. Key to their endeavor was the belief that the human mind can discover the facts and universal laws of nature by means of totally objective observations.

This emphasis on totally objective knowledge has had four significant consequences. First, positivists make a sharp distinction between facts, on the one hand, and feelings and values on the other. They argue that scientists should not let their emotions or values affect their rational processes, for this introduces subjectivity into their conclusions. As Harold Netland points out (1996), they eliminated metaphysics, moral theory, and supernatural realities as "cognitively meaningless"—having no objective validity—because they could not be empirically verified or deduced from empirical propositions.[7] Scientific knowledge was seen as value-neutral; that is, such knowledge might be used to promote a wide variety of values, good or bad, but such knowledge is not biased for or against the realization of any particular values. In other words, positivistic science is concerned with what is, not with what is ethically right.[8] Scientists have often failed to take the moral consequences of their findings into account in deciding whether or not to pursue a particular course of research.

A second consequence of this search for objectivity has been the rise of individualism in modern thought. In the Middle Ages, authority was a central epistemological category, located in tradition (the church, the theologian, the Bible). Positivism relocated it in the individual as an autonomous and ontological being. It is the individual who has the epistemological authority to judge truth and error because only individuals are "real." As Steven Fuller points out, after Descartes it was important that the scientist "withdraw from all social intercourse as a means of getting into the right frame of mind for posing foundational questions about the nature of knowledge" (1991:3). To say that scientific knowledge is produced by sociological processes was thought to discredit it.

A third consequence of this stress on objective knowledge as the only true knowledge was the rejection of all systems of "traditional" knowledge as superstition. Other cultures have no "science" and can be ignored as "primitive." Western thought before the fifteenth century was prelogical and had nothing significant to offer to science. The result was a modern intellectual ethnocentrism that "assumes the intrinsic inferiority of all premodern thought and the consequent superiority of modern thought" (Oden 1992:36). Rarely in history have past and other knowledge systems been so thoroughly rejected.[9]

Finally, to be objective, scientific knowledge had to be seen as an acultural and ahistorical system of knowledge. Houston Smith notes:

> Science capitalizes on this freedom from context and tries to show us a contextless world, a view of things that is not affected by even that fact that it derives from our human angle of vision. And when it goes on to try to understand human beings (through the social sciences), this goal continues (1982:116).

This claim of objective, context-free knowledge faced a problem internal to science itself. The theories scientists teach today are often discarded by newer theories tomorrow. To preserve their faith in the objectivity of their knowledge systems, scientists periodically reinterpret their past views to fit present findings. Textbooks are written to present scientific knowledge as timeless, culture-free truth (Polanyi 1957). Theories and data once accepted as fact are condemned as unscientific or are mercifully forgotten. But as scientific history is constantly reinterpreted, the textbooks themselves must soon be rejected. There is nothing so worthless as outdated textbooks.

Representational Symbols and Algorithmic Logic

To record scientific knowledge objectively, scientists needed precise, culture-free languages that could picture the world accurately—a neutral, theory-free observational *lingua franca* that can be used to formulate scientific theories.

The first exact and totally rational language to emerge was mathematics. It was seen as acultural and ahistorical in character. Scientists were astonished at their ability to predict natural phenomena in mathematical terms. For example, the equation $d = \frac{1}{2}gt^2$ measures exactly how far an object falls over a given period of time in a vacuum on earth; and from it, many of the formulas regarding moving bodies can be generated. Similarly, $e = mc^2$ gives us the amount of energy produced when matter is converted to energy. The experimental results fit mathematical equations so closely that many scientists thought that the order in the universe is a mathematical order.

But mathematics is a limited sign system, and scientists needed a precise language to describe the world. Ordinary languages are too ambiguous, sloppy, and changing. Consequently, scientists such as Rudolph Carnap (1958) and Bertrand Russell (1918–1919) sought to create exact spoken languages that would accurately capture the nature of reality. Scientific words were seen not as arbitrary symbols but as exact (mathematical) representations of reality. Even philosophical speculation was changed into mathematical equations (Osborne 1991).

Meaning in the formal language of science was thought to lie in precisely defined words that refer to (name) or represent real objects (Figure 1). Words were seen not as arbitrary symbols but as exact (mathematical) representations of reality—as depicting "the way things are."

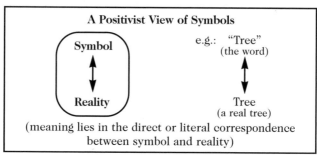

Figure 1

Most positivists were convinced that precise representational symbols made it possible for them to understand theories other than their own. This translatability, or commensurability, made it possible for them to choose rationally between competing theories—a view crucial to their belief that scientific knowledge is progressive. Moreover, scientific knowledge could be translated into other ordinary languages, such as Russian or Japanese, so long as the technical language (e.g., mathematics) remained the same.

To determine truth, positivistic scientists need not only precise languages; they also need an exact rationality based on axiomatic rules. These rules are based on some form of algorithm: they are propositional in nature, mechanical in application, unambiguous in sense, and capable of invariably producing a unique outcome. David Harvey points out:

> From this [perspective]... the world could be controlled and rationally ordered if we could only picture

and represent it rightly. But this presumed that there existed a single correct mode of representation which, if we could uncover it (and this was what scientific and mathematical endeavours were all about), would provide the means to Enlightenment ends (1990:27).

In this form of reasoning, given the same propositions, everyone will come to the same conclusions.

By means of facts and axiomatic reason, scientists sought to formulate precise, consistent, falsifiable theories that are capable of predicting hitherto unknown phenomena, fruitful in reducing disparate phenomena to the same explanatory categories, and capable of solving more problems than did their predecessors and rivals.

Underlying this view of rationality is the assumption that there is one universal system of reason common to all humanity. The rules of logical inquiry are the same in Africa and India as well as in the West. The fact that other cultures have other "logics" does not call this assumption into question. Rather, it shows that other people have yet to acquire positivist knowledge. In other words, they are "prelogical" and "primitive."[10]

Photographic Views of Knowledge and
Grand Unifying Theories

Positivistic science is based on the assumption that scientists, by means of instruments and senses, can gain an accurate, objective knowledge of reality. In other words, scientific terms such as "atoms" and "DNA" refer to real objects in nature; they are not just our mental images. Scientific knowledge is seen as a photograph or literal picture of reality in which information is additive (the whole is the sum of the parts), and scientific statements correspond one-to-one to reality.

If knowledge is additive, the task of science is like erecting a building. Early scientists laid the foundations. We build on these by adding bricks of facts to the walls of knowledge. Once laid, bricks are permanent parts of the structure. Every piece of information must be accurate for the whole theory to be true. An error in any fact or deduction discredits the whole system of knowledge.

According to this view, knowledge is potentially exhaustive, and all problems are solvable in principle. There are no gaps that can ultimately resist the probing of the human mind. In the last decade of the nineteenth century, many physical scientists felt that all the significant problems posed by nature had been solved and that all the fundamental principles of the physical world were known. The 1898–99 catalogue of the University of Chicago stated:

> While it is never safe to affirm that the future of Physical Science has no marvels in store even more astonishing than those of the past, it seems probable that most of the grand underlying principles have been firmly established and that further advances are to be sought chiefly in the rigorous application of these principles to all the phenomena which come under our notice (Schilling 1973:45).[11]

Central to positivist theory is the idea of progress—of faith in human reason to gain control of all areas of life.[12] Scientific knowledge is seen as cumulative as new facts are discovered and better theories formulated. This cumulation is progressive because the scientists assumed that later theories could do everything their predecessors do and more.

The goal of modern science is to build one Grand Unified Theory (GUT) that accounts for all of reality in terms of unchanging, universal principles. For example, in physics there is an ongoing search for a single theory that accounts for the four major forces in nature—gravity, electromagnetism, strong force, and weak force. Another example is the unity-of-science movement that was committed to the reduction of sciences like biology and chemistry to physics.[13] To be useful, a GUT must be powerful (potentially be able to explain all reality), logical (have no internal rational inconsistencies), and autonomous (have no need for causes or factors outside the system). It presupposes that the human mind is capable of exploring all realities and acquiring all knowledge. This idea of universal knowledge leaves no room for a sense of mystery. It also assumes that intellectual harmony will one day be achieved without regard to differences in cultures.

The explosion of knowledge has made it increasingly difficult for science to maintain a single unified theory of reality. Specialization became essential because no human mind can keep up with the rapid developments in knowledge. The result is an increasing fragmentation of knowledge. Fields develop their own working assumptions, vocabularies, criteria for what is true and false, and canons of literature that define the accepted knowledge in the community of scholars involved in those fields. The result is a rapid increase in knowledge but also an inability to reduce all scientific knowledge to one comprehensive system.

Given the explosion of scientific knowledge and the lack of a unifying theory, it should not surprise us that science has been fragmented into what Clifford Geertz (1965:97) calls a stratigraphic approach to knowledge. This recognizes several distinct levels of analysis, each working separately from the others, superimposed on those beneath it, and underpinning those above.[14] For example, when we analyze human beings, we see them as creatures of culture. Strip off the motley forms of culture and we find the structural regularities of social organization. Peel these off and we find the underlying psychological needs—"basic human needs"—such as the need to belong, to have identity and status, and to be creative. Take off the psychological factors and we are left with biological needs—food, shelter, and medical care—that underlie the whole edifice of human life. As we peel off layer after layer, each complete and irreducible in itself, we find another, quite different sort of layer of needs underneath.[15] In the end, this stratified approach to knowledge is fragmented and reductionistic. Ideas and feelings are reduced to chemical changes, and these to the movement of lifeless particles. All knowledge is based on atomic facts. The result is a radical materialism that rejects higher level phenomena as truly real.[16] Today, belief in the unity of scientific knowledge rests not so much on the emergence of a unified theory, but in the faith that the scientific method that underlies all science will eventually provide a common body of knowledge that is internally consistent and powerful.

Disagreements

The emergence of competing theories in naive realism leads to direct confrontations. Two photographs taken of the same object from the same place should be the same. If they differ, only one can be true. Similarly, two different theories in science cannot be held regarding the same reality. In both cases, disagreements lead to controversy and accusations of misobservation or bad reasoning. Positivism is characterized by attacks and counterattacks as each party claims to have the truth.

Positivism and Anthropology

The social sciences emerged as scientists began to study human beings and their sociocultural systems. At first, most scholars studied Western societies, but as they became increasingly aware of the world beyond the West, they invented anthropology as the science of "Others" and "Otherness." The age of exploration brought Europe into contact with a great many different humanlike creatures. Two questions arose: Were these humans, and, if so, how can we explain their differences?[17] The answers were given in the first Grand Unified Theory of anthropology, namely, evolution. This postulated that these strangers were humans, but they were in different stages of biological and cultural progress. Key to this theory was the concept of "civilization," defined as modern life based on positive knowledge, science, and advanced technology. Because Europeans had it, they were seen as educated, rational, and scientific; the Others were ignorant, superstitious, and unscientific. Their Otherness had no validity in its own right. It was defined only in contrast to modernity. Religion was believed to displace the magic of prelogical minds, and science the religions of proto-logical minds. In this light, the colonial venture was not oppressive; it was the West's benevolent endeavor to help the Others join them in their full humanity.

The central task of anthropology was to study strange people who have very strange customs. Specifically, it was to study small, simple societies with low levels of technology, no writing, and tribal religions. Anthropologists did this using the categories, logic, and goals of modernity, which confirmed their beliefs that these societies were primitive and magical in their ways of thinking.

Positivism, Modernity, and Colonialism

The ties between positivism and modernity are close. The term "modern" has an old history, but what Juergen Habermas calls the *project* of modernity came into focus during the eighteenth century.

> That project amounted to an extraordinary intellectual effort on the part of Enlightenment thinkers "to develop objective science, universal morality and law, and autonomous art according to their inner logic."...
> The scientific domination of nature promised freedom from scarcity, want, and the arbitrariness of natural calamity (Harvey 1990:12).

Modernity is built on positivism and the technological knowledge it generated. As Peter Berger and Thomas Luckmann (1966) and Jacques Ellul (1964) point out, the whole of modern society is based on a mechanist model of organization built on the algorithmic logic of positivism. Modernity appeals to the image of rationality incorporated in the machine. Modernity builds factories in which nature is shaped to fit human desires; it forms bureaucracies in which people are treated as interchangeable objects. Rational order, control, efficiency, production, and profit become primary values. The result is the commodification and commercialization of much of life. The result, too, is the rise of specialization as scientific knowledge and technology exploded.

A second connection between positivism and modernity is the division of reality into two separate and largely unrelated realms, natural and supernatural. On the one hand there is the spiritual realm in which God and other spirit beings live and act. This is the world of religion. On the other hand there is the natural realm—the material world of science (Hiebert 1994:189ff.). As Lesslie Newbigin points out, the latter became public facts, taught to everyone; the former was increasingly a matter of private faith (1991). The result was the secularization of the natural domain by the demystification and desacralization of knowledge, a secularism that continues to spread around the world with modernity despite resistance from religious communities.

A third connection is individualism. Positivism is based on the individual's search for truth, and capitalist versions of modernity are based on the individual pursuit of self-achievement and fulfillment. Late modernity, in particular, has stressed competitive individualism as the central value in an entrepreneurial culture (Harvey 1990:171).

A fourth link is faith in progress and evolution. Like positivism, modernity embraces faith in the inevitability of technological development moving onward and upward into the unknown. It stresses the planning of large unified technological and social systems by means of the rationalization and standardization of knowledge and production.

This belief in progress leads modernity to stress cultural uniformity. Other cultures can be discounted as primitive and backward. In time, their people will abandon their old ways and join in the melting pot of modernity. The result of this assimilation is a homogeneous, global culture.

Positivism and modernity are closely tied to Western colonialism. Modern technology made exploration and conquest possible. Positivism justified imperialism and colonial rule. Many Europeans argued that other people are children who need the care and nurture of European adults. This justified their acting as parents, managing the natives' wealth for the natives' own good.

Positivism and Christianity

Christians live in particular historical and cultural contexts. They seek to root their beliefs in the self-revelation of God in history as this is recorded in the Bible, but this does not preclude the fact that their reading of Scripture is deeply influenced by the cultures and times in which they live. It should not surprise us that the theologians and missionaries of the nineteenth and twentieth centuries were influenced by modern science and its positivist epistemological foundations. Many came to see theology itself as a kind of science. For example, W. L. Alexander (1888:1:1) defined systematic theology as "the science of God... a summary of religious truth scientifically arranged." A. H. Strong defined theology as "the science of God and of the relationships between God and the universe" (1972:1). More recently, R. B. Griffiths (1980:169–70) has sought to show that theology is, indeed, a science.

For most of these, to say that theology is a kind of science meant that theology is an orderly and systematic pursuit of knowledge. In this they were emulating the philosophers who used the term in its old Latin sense as *scientia*, meaning knowledge. After the seventeenth century and the emergence of modern science, however, the term "science" came to have another, more restricted meaning. It was equated with "positive" knowledge about the natural world based on empirical observation. Physics and chemistry, which became known as the "hard sciences," served as the models for all other sciences with regard to their rational presuppositions, empirical foundations, and logical rigor reflected in their use of mathematics.

Rudolf Bultmann (1958) tried to make theology fit the modern sciences.[18] Others had little interest in science as a system; they argued that theology must be theology and must chart its own course. However, even they could not ignore the growth of scientific knowledge or the fact that science, not theology, is setting the agenda for the modern world.

Moreover, most Western theologians, missionaries, and Christians have in varying degrees bought into the modern scientific worldview, and what happens in science affects their beliefs in other areas of their lives. It should not surprise us that the epistemological foundations of modernity helped shape those of theology and mission.

Positivism and Theology

Many Protestant theologians, like most scientists, do not examine their epistemological foundations. It should not surprise us, therefore, that many of them are influenced by the successes and apparently solid epistemological foundations of modern science.

Rational Unified System

Systematic theology arose in the twelfth century along with the medieval university (cf. Finger 1985:18–29). Peter Lombard, Thomas Aquinas, and their successors applied the rediscovered philosophical methods of Aristotle to organize theological knowledge as a comprehensive system of thought organized around questions of the nature of unchanging, eternal realities that is logically consistent and internally coherent. These questions had earlier dominated Greek philosophy. Apparent inconsistencies (and too often mysteries) were taken as proof of error. Truth was determined by rational argument and was encoded in propositional statements that were linked together by reason. This was particularly true of Protestant theologians who were trying to break with the Roman Catholic appeal to tradition. Max Weber notes:

> With Calvin the *decretum horribile* is derived not, as with Luther, from religious experience, but from the logical necessity of his thought; therefore its importance increases with every increase in the logical consistency of that religious thought (1958:102).

Underlying this search was a belief that human rationality is based on universal laws of thought. True logic, it was thought, is transcultural, and its model is mathematics with its precise propositions and algorithmic deductions. In such a logical system the exact nature of facts and reason are necessary to construct a true theory. A single error in either calls the whole system into question. Knowledge must be accurate in every detail for the whole to be true.

The goal of modern systematic theology is to present a single, unified picture of truth that is comprehensive and potentially exhaustive. Like modern science, this search for a Grand Unified Theory of fundamental unchanging realities is rooted in Greek philosophy and its search for the universal structures that underlie the flux of life and history. For Christian theologians, biblical history is the data on which they build their theology, but they seek more than a theology that looks for truth in the context of history. They are looking for the unchanging verities that underlie reality.

Objective Truth

A positivist stance in theology postulates a direct (sometimes referred to as one-to-one) correspondence between the Bible and theology—between the messages found in the texts and the interpretation of them in the mind of the theologian, who is seen as an objective observer. It assumes that the careful scholar of the text can understand the meaning intended by the writer accurately and without bias. Hermeneutics consists of a careful reading and comparison of the texts. Questions about the cultural, historical, and personal experiences of the theologian do not enter the picture. Because the Bible is affirmed as true, as it is by conservative theologians, and because theology is seen as an accurate and unbiased reading of the Bible, theology itself becomes absolute truth. Positivist theology claims both biblical authority and theological certitude.

To have true theology, positivists need precise words and exact algorithmic reasoning. They believe that carefully defined terms refer directly to reality; they assume that an accurate use of language can convey precise meanings without loss or distortion. Consequently, many theological debates center around the exact definition of key terms, and faith is defined as understanding and affirming cognitive creedal statements without mental reservation. Feelings and responses are products of theology, not of its essence.

Because theology requires a precise, technical knowledge of the Scriptures and philosophy, it should be done by specialists. The laity are encouraged to study the Bible for themselves, but the orthodoxy of their beliefs is determined by the experts. Systematic theology in this sense "has been an almost entirely western, middle or upper class, male discipline. It has seldom, if ever, been pursued in eastern Christendom or in 'third world' countries" (Finger 1985:28).

Strengths and Weaknesses

A positivist approach to theology has real strengths. First, it has a high view of theology as the foundation on which all life must be lived. It was deep theological convictions that informed and motivated the Reformation and the modern mission movement.

Second, it has a high view of truth and absolutes, and it rejects relativism. It affirms that humans can know the truth through careful study and that this knowledge can save them. A theology faithful to Scripture is essential to knowing God and living a godly life.

Finally, this approach to theology affirms the oneness of humankind and the underlying unity of human reason. In so doing, it affirms commensurability—that God can communicate with humans, and, therefore, humans can understand and communicate with one another. Underlying the differences of culture and history, we are one humanity.

Theology based on positivism also has its weaknesses. First, it does not differentiate sufficiently between divine revelation recorded in Scripture and theology as a human endeavor that seeks to understand that revelation. It often claims final authority for theology, which belongs to Scripture alone. One particular danger here is that of absolutizing uncertain doctrines—those the Bible does not clearly teach—to certain truth. There is no place for possible or even probable truth, and no place for mystery (Osborne 1996). In seeking to affirm truth, positivism is in danger of ignoring our finiteness and of worshiping the human mind.

Second, theology in this mode seeks to understand the eternal, universal structure of reality. In so doing, it is in danger of ignoring the importance of history as the basis of God's work and self-revelation. In its search for unchanging truth, it often ignores the unfolding nature of divine truth reveled in Scripture, the Story of God's deeds. T. F. Torrance writes:

> Hellenistic thought operated with a radical dichotomy between a realm of ideas and a realm of events, and it took its stand within the realm of ideas as the realm of the ultimately real. From this perspective it could only regard the Christian doctrines of God at work in history, of the coming of the Son of God into human and creaturely existence, of the Eternal entering the world of space and time, as unreal, or at best as a "mythological" way of expressing certain timeless truths (1978:17).

Moreover, theology often does not address the problems of everyday human life that are in constant flux, nor does it lead to a passion for missions that arises from our encounter with real people who are lost.

Third, in its emphasis on objective knowledge, positivist theology appears to many to be a dry exercise with little place for feelings and morals. It looks for orthodoxy more than orthopraxy and defines the former mainly in terms of cognitive correctness. It assumes that once people have the right knowledge, they will live according to it. It does not define faith as a personal response to God's salvation that manifests itself in the form of obedience and transformed lives.

Fourth, positivism brings into theology the strong individualism that characterizes modernity. The search for truth and salvation is a personal matter and does not include the church as a hermeneutical community.   Proper theology should be done by experts, not by laity.

Fifth, positivism with its notion of progress gave rise to theologies that equated the Kingdom of God with the utopia being created by science and Christian morality, a utopia that will wipe out famine, oppression, and war and will restore the world to a pristine society. In so doing, the center of theology moved from God and his activities to humans and their efforts (Bosch 1991:313–41).

Finally, disagreements in this theological stance often lead to conflicts. From the view of naive realism, there can be only one right theology. If there are disagreements, one of the theologies must be false. Because each of us assumes that we are reading the biblical text honestly and without bias, we judge others as mistaken. Disagreements often lead to direct confrontations, accusations of heresy, and schisms in the church. There is little room to work together to understand Scriptures and to live with differences in the body of Christ.

Theology and Science

One central question facing modern Christians is the relationship between theology and science. The division of reality into two domains—supernatural and natural—has led to a chasm between religion and science. In modern thought, the former deals with spiritual realities and ultimate matters, which are beyond our immediate observation. Consequently, religion is often thought to be based on "faith" alone. The only places spiritual realities impinge on the material world are in creation and in miracles that transcend or violate the laws of nature. Science, on the other hand, describes our material world and makes humans the lords of nature. It does not need faith because science is based on "hard facts."

Given this view, the integration of theology and science into a single, comprehensive system of explanation is difficult. The simplest solution is reductionism. Here all phenomena are ultimately reduced to a single explanatory system. Scientific reductionism reduces religion to social and psychological functions. Theological reductionism attributes all human problems, such as illnesses, to spiritual causes and refuses to go to science for answers. In the end, reductionism achieves integration between theology and science by denying the validity of one or the other of them.

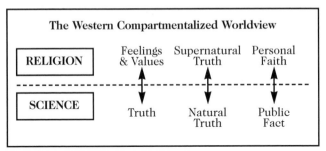

Figure 2

A second way to integrate positivist science and theology is by compartmentalization—by treating them as separate, nonoverlapping systems (Figure 2). Many people argue that whereas science is a matter of facts and truth, religion is a matter of feelings and is the source of deep personal experience. Others assert that religion has to do with morality; it provides people with values that regulate their behavior and so make corporate life possible. Christians, by and large, reject these views. Christianity, they argue, *is* about facts and truth.

Modernity imposes another dualism on us. As Newbigin points out (1989), in the West science is seen as public truth, having to do with the "natural realities" of this world. All students must study mathematics, physics, chemistry, and the social sciences. Religion is seen as a matter of personal truth, having to do with "supernatural realities" such as sin, salvation, miracles, and prophecies. No classes on Christianity, or Islam, or Hinduism that seek to convert students to these religions are required. In fact, they cannot be taught as truth in public schools. This dualism between science and religion, fact and faith, natural order and miracles, body and spirit dominates the worldview of most ordinary Westerners and leads to an otherworldly Christianity and to the secularization of everyday life.

Positivism and Missions

The history of the modern mission movement coincides with the history of Western colonial expansion around the world. It should not surprise us that Western missionaries of that time were often influenced by its philosophical underpinnings—in particular, its positivist epistemological foundations. The ways in which they contextualized (or did not contextualize) the gospel, responded to the theological pluralism in non-Western churches, and related to non-Christian religions were determined to a great extent by their epistemological premises.

Before examining the epistemological assumptions of these missionaries, we must first recognize their greatness. A strong sense of the truth and the certainty of their theological convictions drove many of them to the ends of the earth at the cost of their lives. They were convinced that humans without salvation were eternally lost and that Christ was the only path to that salvation. The result was the great missionary movement that planted churches in the most remote regions of the earth and led to the conversion of hundreds of millions of people from most tongues, tribes, and nations. There were few areas of the world where the gospel was not proclaimed. There is no question that God worked mightily through them, human though they were, to plant the church around the world.

Christianity and Civilization

A positivist view of missions had its problems. Most Protestant missionaries of the nineteenth and early twentieth centuries were convinced not only of the truthfulness of Christianity but also of the superiority of Western "civilization."[19] Charles Taber notes:

> The superiority of Western civilization as the culmination of human development, the attribution of that superiority to the prolonged dominance of Christianity, the duty of Christians to share civilization and the gospel with the "benighted heathen"—these were the chief intellectual currency of their lives (1991:71).

Wilbert Shenk writes:

> The seventeenth-century New England Puritan mis-
> sionaries largely set the course for modern missions....
> The model by which they measured their converts
> was English Puritan civilization.... They gathered
> these new Christians into churches for nurture and
> discipline and set up programs to transform Christian
> Indians into English Puritans (1980:35).

This attitude of Western intellectual superiority had its roots
in the ideas of progress and "manifest destiny" in which both
Christianity and science worked together to contribute to
the betterment of the world morally and materially (Bosch
1991:298–302). Missionaries believed themselves to be par-
ticipating in a worldwide crusade of human advancement.
They built schools and hospitals alongside churches and
taught science as an essential part of the curriculum along
with the gospel. In many parts of the world, Christianity
became equated with Western civilization and commerce,
and the reshaping of the entire world in the image of "modernity" was seen as a foregone conclusion.

The expansion of Western trade led to the conquest of new
lands and the establishment of colonies and imperial rule.
The relationship between Christian missions and colonialism
was a strained one. On the one hand, most missionaries went
to their nation's colonies—German missionaries to German
colonies, British missionaries to British colonies—and many
welcomed colonial rule because it gave them protection and
access to these lands. The imperial rulers at first opposed
missionary activities, fearing that these would upset the people and hinder trade and rule, but many came to view missionaries as allies in pacifying and civilizing the "natives."
David Bosch points out:

> Few mission advocates... challenged the attitude
> prevalent among Western Christians of the period,
> namely, where their power went there was the place to
> send their missionaries, or the corollary, where they

have sent their missionaries there their power should
go (1991:306).

Missionaries were expected to remain patriotic to their countries, and few sided with the nationalist movements that
emerged in many colonies in the twentieth century.
Moreover, most nationals saw missionaries as closely allied
with colonial powers. On the other hand, as Lamin Sanneh
points out (1993), missionaries often sided with the people
in conflicts with the imperial rulers.

It should not surprise us, given their view of civilization,
progress, and divine destiny, that traders, rulers, and missionaries alike were paternalistic in their attitudes toward
the local people. Although missionaries recognized early the
need to turn over authority and power to native leaders, by
the end of the nineteenth century they argued that this tran-
sition must wait until these leaders were at least as well educated and experienced as the missionaries they displaced.
Bosch writes:

> The enthusiastic discussions about "self-governing,
> self-expanding, and self-supporting churches," so
> prominent around the middle of the nineteenth cen-
> tury, were for all practical purposes shelved by the
> beginning of the twentieth. The younger churches
> had, almost unnoticed, been demoted from churches
> in their own right to mere "agents" of the missionary
> societies (1991:295).

Measured by the standards of "civilization," other cultures were seen as prelogical and primitive. Their customs
and beliefs could therefore be ignored, for it was clear that in
time their people would be enlightened by modern education
and would reject their old ways. John Pobee writes:

> The historical churches by and large implemented the
> doctrine of *tabula rasa*, i.e., the missionary doctrine
> that there is nothing in the non-Christian culture on
> which the Christian missionary can build and, therefore,
> every aspect of the traditional non-Christian culture

had to be destroyed before Christianity could be built up (1982:169).

Native churches not only had little to learn from their own cultures; those cultures were also seen as pagan. Consequently, the task of missions was not to contextualize the gospel in the local culture but to displace it with Christian ways. These ways were defined in terms of Western Christian practices. Most converts were encouraged to leave their old ways and become Western. The result was an unnecessary foreignness of the gospel. The gospel *is* foreign to every culture, for it is God's prophetic voice calling sinners and the societies and cultures they create to repent and be transformed. But missionaries often added to this the foreignness of Western culture—of dress, architecture, pews, translated hymns, Western leadership styles, and imported technology. Those who became Christians were often seen as traitors to their own cultures.

The Gospel

Positivism defined the missionaries' gospel in several important ways. First, it divorced the cognitive from the affective and moral dimensions of life, and defined the gospel largely in terms of knowledge. This is reflected in the name of one of the first mission agencies, the Society for the Propagation of Christian Knowledge. Moreover, the missionaries sought to demonstrate the superiority of Christianity over other religions on the basis of reason. As E. Stanley Jones notes (1925:141), many saw themselves as God's lawyers.

Second, positivism led to formal equivalence translations of the Bible. Meaning was thought to lie in precise words that correspond directly with reality. Consequently, Bible translation consisted of the accurate translation of words from one language to another. These translations often lost the meanings of the original texts because they did not take into account the contextual nature of every language. Nevertheless, as Sanneh points out (1993), the very act of translating the Bible into local languages gave the people the power to read and interpret it for themselves. Probably no other factor in modern missions has played so important a role in the emergence of autonomous national churches.

Third, influenced by positivism, missionaries established schools for the training of leaders in which the acquisition of knowledge was seen as the central qualification for ministry.[20] Most missionaries believed that there is only one correct body of knowledge—only one true theology—and that this had to be transmitted unchanged to their students. Because only one theology could be true, other theological views had to be condemned as error. Moreover, there was little room for local churches to develop their own theologies. To many nationalistically minded leaders, this was theological colonialism.

Fourth, the Supernatural/Natural dualism implicit in the Greek and positivist worldviews deeply influenced mission thought. It led to the division between "evangelism" and the "social gospel," and to an unending debate about the relationship between the two. It also led many missionaries to see their task as twofold: as evangelism and church planting to Christianize the people, and as building schools and hospitals to civilize them. The latter were often seen as tools to achieve the former. Their curricula and medicines, however, were based primarily on the sciences. Courses on the Bible were taught and prayer meetings held before medical work began, but these often reinforced the fact that science was seen as the answer to "natural" problems. It should not surprise us that many people adopted the science we brought but rejected our Christianity.

Other Religions

A positivist evangelical view of Christianity strongly affirms the truth and uniqueness of Christ and the gospel, and rejects all other religions as false. Conversion, therefore, requires a total displacement of the old religion by the new. Because meaning in a system of knowledge is the sum of its parts, none of the ideas and practices of the old religion can be used in indigenous expressions of Christian faith, for these will poison the whole. Moreover, because in most societies all areas of life have religious significance, few local symbols and customs could be used in the church. For example, in India it was the custom for Hindu women to use red saris at their weddings to symbolize fertility. Many missionaries rejected red because it was used by Hindus and substituted white, even though in India, white symbolized barrenness and death. Similarly, in many parts of the world dramas were prohibited because they were used in the native religions. The result was a confrontational approach to other religions.

Attacks on Positivism

Positivism has changed the world for good. It has a strong sense of truth and order, and a high view of nature. By focusing attention on careful empirical research, it gave rise to modern science, which has contributed greatly to our understanding of the world, and to technologies that have benefited life on earth. It is hard for us today to imagine what life was like in the West before modernity.

But positivism is also flawed. It has divorced knowledge from morality and feelings, and in so doing it has unleashed modern technology with few moral constraints, and power without safeguards. In its materialistic forms it has absolutized scientific knowledge and relegated religion to private opinion, and it reduces humans to robots in a mechanistic world. Today the certainty of positivism and the optimism that marked its early years have been undermined from within and from without. Positivism is no longer accepted as universally true.

Internal Attacks

Attacks against positivism came, in part, from within science itself. As scientists began to use scientific methods to study science and the scientific process, they began to question some of its fundamental assumptions.

Attacks Against Objectivism

The first major assumption to be questioned was that of unbiased objectivism. Classical physics based on Newtonian and Kantian concepts of time and space were called into question by Einstein in the theory of relativity and by Bohr in quantum mechanics.[21] Their theories showed that scientists are very much a part of the picture they observe. The vantage point from which scientists make their observations inevitably shapes their observations. The discovery of non-Euclidian geometries and non-Cantorian algebra shattered the supposed unity of mathematical language. The idea that there is only one possible way to represent reality began to break down.

Second, the social sciences, when applied to the study of scientists and science, showed that scientists are deeply influenced by their historical and cultural contexts. Psychologists destroyed the notions of unbiased observation, and of the mind either as a passive recipient and reflector of sensory information or as an observer with innate mental categories with which to organize sense experiences. Linguists such as A. Korzybski (1994) and Ludwig Wittgenstein (1953) showed us that the language in which we encode knowledge is itself a cultural creation. Moreover, the order perceived by scientists is, in part, shaped by the categories they create. It became clear that all languages rest on theoretical presuppositions, and, in Russell Hanson's oft-quoted words, "all data are theory-laden." By the 1940s and 1950s, the idea of a neutral observation language had been discarded. It was taken as self-evident that every body of knowledge, including every scientific theory, has its own language.

Anthropologists and sociologists raised further questions. Peter Berger and Thomas Luckmann (1966) and Karl Mannheim (1952) showed that scientists are influenced by the scientific communities of which they are a part, and there is no value-free or power-free knowledge Anthropologists demonstrated that scientists themselves are molded by their own cultural and historical contexts. In other words, there can be no culture-free human knowledge—no transcendental knower who is able to know without affecting the known. All knowledge emerges in particular cultural and historical settings. This makes science a Western mind game.

Anthropologists also raised questions about the status of the reality of human ideas and cultures. The natural scientists observe a material world that they observe through their senses and instruments. Social scientists study other people—their beliefs, feelings, and values. As Marvin Harris points out (1980:38), the social scientist has to deal with four types of reality (Figure 3). It is clear that these are not all equally true; not all will survive rigorous examination. Nevertheless, all are real in the sense that they are the ways certain persons (people or scientists) take to be real. Nor can we assume that the scientist is always right and the people always wrong, as positivists would have it.

The ontological and epistemological statuses of sectors 1 and 4 create the thorniest problems. The scientist has well-developed methods, including photography and tape recording, to determine what, in fact, empirically happens in a situation. People, on the other hand, are best able to say what they think. But what happens when the people see or claim to see something, such as a demon, and the scientist does not (sector 1)? Or can the scientist claim to know what is going on in the minds of the people, which they deny or of which they themselves are unconscious (sector 4)? Some scientists argue that the introduction of emic realities relativizes all human knowledge and makes it impossible to have a social science that seeks objective truth.

Types of Human Reality		
	EMIC	ETIC
Behavioral	1 What the people see or say they see	2 What the scientist sees or says he/she sees
Mental	3 The explanation the people give of what they see	4 The explanation the scientist gives of what he/she sees

Figure 3

Philosophers and historians of science like Kurt Gödel, Michael Polanyi, and Thomas Kuhn critiqued the rational assumptions underlying positivism. Gödel (1992) proved that it is impossible to have a Grand Unified Theory that is (1) strong, (2) autonomous, and (3) logically consistent. Only two of these are possible in any given human theory. Polanyi (1957) points out the important distinction between knowledge acquired through the senses and knowledge that depends on the mind's search for order and meaning. He notes that even if we could accurately observe the world and record these observations in a language with total accuracy and without bias, and even "if we did succeed *per impossibile* in keeping track of the elements of mental behavior without reference to mind, these particulars observed in themselves would remain meaningless and experiments conducted with these meaningless fragments would also be meaningless" (cited in Nott 1971:154). Reduced to purely empirical statements, science could only make statements such as, "It is a fine day; by which we mean the sun is shining, the air is 72 degrees Fahrenheit, there is a slight breeze blowing, and the air is fresh." History would be reduced to descriptive statements about the nature and sequence of events. There would be no "explanation" of them, no "story" to tell.

Kuhn (1970) and Paul Feyerabend (1970) took this contextualization of knowledge systems a step further and argued that scientists advocating one theory cannot accurately understand competing theories; theories are incommensurable. Consequently, choices between them cannot be made on the basis of evidence and reason. Scientific theories "proven true" at one time are often later rejected as false. Science is, therefore, not a growing body of verified laws built on indisputable facts, but a series of competing paradigms, no one of which can be shown to be true. This undermined the sine qua non for scientific rationality and with it belief in the truth and progress of scientific knowledge. The social sciences, in particular, felt the impact of their critique.

The net result of these attacks on positivism was to take science from its privileged vantage point outside and above history and culture, and to place it squarely in the middle of human subjectivity. James Brown writes:

> It is part of our situation that we are inevitably and inseparably *inside* the knowledge relation, from the start to the end, and so cannot step outside of ourselves to an indifferent standpoint from which to view and adjust the relations of thought and being (1955:170).

In the light of our current understandings, human knowledge can no longer be equated literally with reality. This does not mean the end of realism. It does mean that a new and humbler form of it is needed.

Attacks Against Determinism

The notable successes of the physical sciences in explaining external realities in terms of mechanistic, deterministic paradigms have led many social scientists to extend the paradigm to human beings. Among the current forms are Skinnerian behavioralism and modern sociobiology.

Scholars have challenged metaphysical determinism on several grounds. First, it has limited applicability. It best explains observations of lifeless matter. It is least able to predict human behavior in day-to-day living. Few would argue that a scientist should not use determinism as a research strategy if this provides us with insights into the nature of humans. The question is, Can it be used to explain everything about human beings? Are they not more than programmed machines?

Second, mechanistic science is reflexive. Positive scientists assume that scientists are nonreflexive subjects; that is, they do not apply their methods to examine themselves (Fuller 1991:188). However, in studying humans social scientists *are* indirectly studying themselves. If determinism applies to humans, it also applies to scientists, reducing their theories to heredity, child-rearing practices, or what they ate for dinner. It is questionable whether people who employ deterministic principles in formulating their theories can themselves be understood solely within the framework of these same deterministic principles.

External Attacks

The external attacks against positivism deal largely with the impact of modernity on humankind. It has failed to produce the utopia it promised and has failed to offer real succor in human crises. After World War II, scholars began to ask why humankind, far from advancing toward harmony, had sunk into the abyss of hitherto unimaginable barbarism. Why had science served the cause of cruelty? Pauline Rosenau notes:

> Modernity entered history as a progressive force promising to liberate humankind from ignorance and irrationality, but one can readily wonder whether that promise has been sustained. As we in the West approach the end of the twentieth century, the "modern" record—world wars, the rise of Nazism, concentration camps (in both East and West), genocide, worldwide depression, Hiroshima, Vietnam, Cambodia, the Persian gulf, and a widening gap between rich and poor—makes any belief in the idea of progress or faith in the future seem questionable (1992:5).

One charge leveled against positivism is that it is imperialist in attitude and has led to intellectual colonialism. Clifford Geertz accuses anthropologists of the British Structural Functionalist school of intellectual imperialism and of legitimating and empowering British colonialism of bringing "Africans into a world conceived in deeply English terms, and confirming thereby the domination of those terms" (1988:70). Max Weber argued that the strong linkage Enlightenment thinkers made between the growth of science, rationality, and universal human freedom was a bitter illusion. Their legacy was the triumph of purposive-instrumental rationality. David Harvey asserts:

> [T]he suspicion lurks that the Enlightenment project was doomed to turn against itself and transform the

quest for human emancipation into a system of universal oppression in the name of human liberation....
[The] logic that hides behind Enlightenment rationality is a logic of domination and oppression (1990:13).

A second charge is that positivist science is amoral in character. In an effort to be totally objective, it has excluded both feelings and values from its observations. It describes and explains but does not prescribe. It asks whether a nuclear weapon can be built, but not if it should be built. Consequently, positivism has not provided humankind with the moral foundations for addressing the world's problems. Even so staunch a positivist as Ernest Gellner admits:

The Enlightenment... proposed a secular version of a salvation religion, a naturalistic doctrine of universally valid salvation, in which reason and nature replaced revelation.... The attempt to implement politically this new secular faith failed, twice over; this is the story of the aftermath of both the French and the Russian Revolution, the two great attempts to implement the Enlightenment (1992:90).

Regarding the world scene, David Bosch writes,

The West's grand schemes, at home and in the Third World, have virtually all failed dismally. The dream of a unified world in which all would enjoy peace, liberty, and justice has turned into a nightmare of conflict, bondage, and injustice. The disappointment is so fundamental and pervasive that it cannot possibly be ignored or suppressed (1991:361).

Finally, positivism is charged with intellectual ethnocentrism. It disdains all other systems of knowledge, past and present, and claims for itself alone a knowledge of the truth.

If positivism is flawed, what epistemology can we trust? One answer is offered by postpositivism and postmodernity. We will examine these next to see if they offer us a better way.

2

The Epistemological Challenges of Instrumentalism and Idealism

Forced to leave the comfortable certainty of positivism, many scientists, particularly those in the social sciences, are now looking for new epistemological foundations. What are their options? To answer this question, we need a taxonomy of epistemological systems—a second order model to use Bertrand Russell's phrase—to compare and contrast various epistemological options. There are dangers in creating such a grid. Any taxonomy imposes biases on the field and overlooks the fine nuances of various positions. Moreover, it assumes that epistemological paradigms are commensurable (contra Kuhn 1970 and Lyotard 1984) and that some measure of mutual understanding and comparison between them is possible.

There are, however, greater dangers in looking at various epistemological positions in isolation or of assuming that they are incommensurable. If comparison between epistemological alternatives is impossible, rationality is undermined, and with it science, philosophy, and theology. Extreme postmodernists, in fact, do take this stance, but, as we will see, this leads them to nihilism.

The taxonomy suggested here (Figure 4) is overly simple, but it may help us understand the current crisis in epistemology and some of the current movements, such as postmodernism, of our time. In the last column the various epistemological answers are illustrated by a parable. Several umpires stood talking after a baseball game when a player asked them, "Why did you call that particular pitch a strike?" Each of the umpires gave a different response based on his epistemological position.

A Taxonomy of Epistemological Positions

Position	Nature of Knowledge	Relationship Between Systems of Knowledge	The Umpire's Response
Absolute Idealism	Reality exists in the mind. The external world is illusory (e.g., Vedantic and Advaita Hinduism).	Each system is an island to itself. Systems are incommensurable. Unity is possible only as everyone joins in the same system.	"My calling it a strike makes it a strike. The game is in my mind."
Critical Idealism	Reality exists in the mind. The external world is unknowable. Order is imposed on sense experience by the mind.	Each system is an island to itself. Systems are incommensurable. A common ground is found in human rationality, which is assumed to be the same for all humans.	"My calling it a strike makes is a strike. My mind imposes order on the world."
Naive Idealism/ Naive Realism (Positivism)	The external world is real. The mind can know it exactly, exhaustively, and without bias. Science is a photograph of reality. Knowledge and reality are equated uncritically.	Because knowledge is exact and potentially exhaustive, there can be only one unified theory. Various theories must be reduced to one. This leads to reductionism in the physical, psychological, or sociocultural sphere.	"I call it the way it is. If it is a strike I call it a strike. If it is a ball I call it a ball."
Critical Realism	The external world is real. Our knowledge of it is partial but can be true. Science is a map or model. It is made up of successive paradigms that bring us to closer approximations of reality and absolute truth.	Each field in science presents a different blueprint of reality. These are complementary to one another. Integration is achieved, not by reducing them all to one model, but by seeing their interrelationship. Each gives us partial insights into reality.	"I call it the way I see it, but there is a real pitch and an objective standard against which I must judge it. I can be shown to be right or wrong."

Figure 4

Continued on the following page

Position	Nature of Knowledge	Relationship Between Systems of Knowledge	The Umpire's Response
Instrumentalism (Pragmatism)	The external world is real. We cannot know if our knowledge of it is true, but if it "does the job" we can use it. Science is a Rorschach response that makes no ontological claims to truth.	Because we make no truth claims for our theories or models, there can be no ontological contradictions between them. We can use apparently contradictory models in different situations so long as they work.	"I call it the way I see it, but there is no way to know if I am right or wrong."
Determinism	The external world is real. We and our knowledge are determined by material causes; hence knowledge can lay no claim to truth (or to meaning).	There is no problem with integration, for all systems of knowledge are determined by external, nonrational factors such an infant experiences, emotional drives, and thought conditioning.	"I call it the way I am programmed to."

Figure 4

Source: Paul G. Hiebert. Epistemological foundations for science and theology. *TSF Bulletin*. 8.4 (March–April 1985):5–10. Reprinted in Paul G. Hiebert, *Anthropological Reflections on Missiological Issues*. Grand Rapids: Baker Book House, MI. 1994, 23. Used by permission.

Instrumentalism, Idealism, and Postpositive Science

One response to the collapse of positivism (a form of naive realism) has been to fall back on a more tentative form of realism. The central epistemological problem in the philosophy of science is this: How do we use empirical evidence to make rational choices between rival theories? Positivists argued that these choices are based on reason, for new theories can do all that the old theories do and more. Thomas Kuhn and Willard Quine, trying to demonstrate this in the history of science, came to the conclusion that such decisions are, in fact, not based on hard facts or reason but on social dynamics—on politics and propaganda in which prestige, power, age, and polemics determine the outcome between competing theories. Furthermore, they argue that all scientific theories are underdetermined; in other words, any theory can be reconciled with any evidence, and there never comes a point at which it is "unscientific" to hang on to an old one that is challenged by a new and apparently better one. In the end, the most Kuhn could salvage of realism was to argue that science is a "useful" way of looking at the world because it helps us solve problems. In other words, he and others like him moved to an instrumentalist or postpositivist view of reality.[1]

The Characteristics of Instrumentalism

What are the key tenets of instrumentalism, and how does it solve the problems of reality and truth?

Subjective Realism

First, instrumentalism is a form of realism. It assumes a real external world that we perceive through our senses, but it sees our knowledge of it mainly as a cultural creation. Karl Popper (1959) challenged the positivist assumption of totally objective knowledge when he pointed out that the "facts" of science may themselves be called into question if they do not fit our theories. It is the scientific community that decides which of them are to be considered "solid" and which must be questioned. Kuhn (1970) argued that all "facts" are theory dependent. Their meaning is found only in the larger conceptual framework—the paradigm—of a particular community of scholars. In short, cultural conventionalism enters science at its most basic level. Willard Quine notes:

> The totality of our so-called knowledge or beliefs, from the most casual matters of geography and history to the profoundest laws of atomic physics or even of pure mathematics and logic, is a man-made fabric which impinges on experience only along the edges (1969:413).

Instrumentalism also challenges the separation of cognition from feelings and values. There is no cold, totally objective reasoning. All human thought, it argues, combines ideas, feelings, and judgments in complex ways. Scientific discoveries are charged with high emotions that influence their work. In the end, we are left with knowledge, based on experiences, that is fundamentally subjective in nature.

This growing awareness of the subjective nature of knowledge raises fundamental questions: Can we show that knowledge has any objective dimension to it, and can we distinguish between what in our knowledge is subjective and what is not? If we cannot answer these questions in the affirmative, we will never know when our knowledge is objectively based and when it is not. Moreover, if ideas are creations of our minds, can we speak of them as "true"? Instrumentalists argue that we cannot know when our theories reflect external realities and when they are creations of our paradigms. Consequently, we cannot distinguish between what is objective and what is subjective in our knowledge, and we must, therefore, abandon the concept of truth with regard to our human knowledge (Kuhn 1970).

Diadic Symbols and Algorithmic Logic

Positivism assumes that reality can be accurately encoded in precise symbols. Linguists such as Ludwig Wittgenstein (1953)[2], and J. L. Austin (1962) have shown us that words do not refer directly to realities, as formerly thought. Rather, they are humanly shaped categories that differ markedly from one language to another. In other words, languages are cultural conventions used by people in their conversations. To understand words, we must understand the sentences and paragraphs in which they are found. To understand sentences and paragraphs, we must understand the social situations— the language games—in which they are spoken. Ultimately, words take on meaning in the context of a worldview. Nancy Murphy and James McClendon note:

> Putting it in an oversimplified form, whereas for clas-
> sical Greek thought, ideas determined both reality and
> language, and for moderns, at least with the rise of
> empiricism, experience determined ideas, which
> determined language, in postmodern thought the
> tables are turned and language makes possible both
> ideas and experience (1989:202–203).

This shift in our understanding of the nature of language led to an essentially diadic view of signs (Figure 5). Wilhelm von Humboldt, one of the fathers of linguistics, differentiated between the "inner" and "outer" dimensions of symbols such as words. The former, he said, was the mental concept associated with a word, the latter its oral or written form. His student, Ferdinand de Saussure, labeled these as the *signifian* (signifier or form), and *signifi* (signified or meaning of a word).[3] In this view, the meaning of words is given by their relation to other words and to images in our minds, rather than by their reference to objects. However, as Wittgenstein points out, meanings are not private. They are created and used in social communities. We use words in different kinds of language games to communicate our ideas to others in our culture. This is possible only if we share understandings of reality, at least within a community that shares a common culture. This view limits meaning to subjective mental images and denies that these images have any direct relationship to external realities. In other words, symbols have no objective referents.

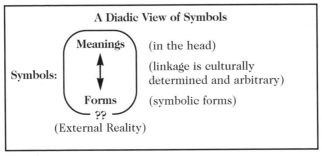

Figure 5

If meaning is found in people's heads, then communication is measured not by the accurate transmission of objective facts, but by the inner images and feelings that are generated in the mind of the listener. Communication, therefore, must be receptor oriented. What is important is not what the sender means but what the listeners perceive.

Distinguishing form and meaning in symbols is an important corrective to the positivist view of signs that equated forms with external realities. First, it shows us that there is an important subjective dimension to human knowledge. People are not just passive recorders of the world around them. Moreover, sender-oriented communication does not guarantee that the people understand the message accurately.

Second, the distinction between forms and meanings makes us aware of how deeply cultures shape languages. Words do not simply denote realities. Words are full of feelings, value judgments, allusions to other things, and other connotative information. Language, in other words, is not surface, precise and flat like mathematics. It is multivocal, rich and full of subtle nuances. This is what makes language so powerful, but this richness also makes it fuzzy and ambiguous.

Paradigms and Rorschach Views of Knowledge

Thomas Kuhn, in his analysis of the history of science, argues that knowledge is paradigmatic. By this he means that it is not simply the sum of facts. It is paradigmatic or configurational— a mentally created image that gives meaning to the facts by interpreting them and providing coherence to the whole. For this reason, Kuhn is referred to as a "constructivist."

For a somewhat simple example of what is meant by paradigm, we look at the dots in Figure 6, and we "see a star." Others may see two circles. It is this mental organization of bits of information that gives them meaning by linking them into an explanatory interpretation.

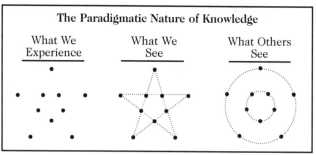

Figure 6

If scientific theories are paradigmatic in nature, then the history of science is not linear and cumulative. As Kuhn points out, it is a sequence of paradigms, each competing and replacing the one before it in what amounts to a scientific revolution. One paradigm does not evolve into the other. For example, the Ptolemaic theory of planets was replaced by that of Copernicus, and this, in turn, by Einstein's relative space.

Because knowledge is made up of our inner images of "reality," it is partial and fragmented. We develop knowledge to solve specific problems we face. We have theories about the physical world, about life, about human beings, about building skyscrapers, about baking cakes, and about raising children. In instrumentalism we do not need to organize these systems of belief into one coherent picture of reality, as positivists seek to do. Nor do we need to worry when these systems contradict one another, because we are not making truth claims for any of them. In this sense, instrumentalism is nonreductionistic. It can accept different theories about different realities without forcing them into one coherent picture. It also does not claim to be exhaustive. There is no need to know everything in order to understand a part of our human experience.

If knowledge is paradigmatic, can people in one paradigm understand and communicate with those in another one? Kuhn argues no—paradigms are incommensurable. All knowledge claims (facts, truth, and validity) are intelligible and debatable only in the context and community of a paradigm. Regarding paradigms, Paul Feyerabend writes:

> Their content cannot be compared. Nor is it possible to make a judgment of verisimilitude except within the confines of a particular theory.... What remains are subjective judgments, judgments of taste, and our own subjective wishes (1970:228).

Because there is no neutral observation language and because there are no translation manuals for rival theoretical languages, communication between people in different scientific paradigms is impossible. In fact, they cannot intelligently understand one another. They simply talk past each other. Rival theories become not merely different ways of looking at reality, but different worlds and different realities.

One casualty of incommensurability is truth. If it is impossible rationally to compare different systems of knowledge and to show that one theory is better than another, there is no way to affirm that one theory is closer to the truth than the other.[4] Quine asserts that "any theory can be held true, come what may," and I. Lacatos holds that any theory can be made to look good, provided enough bright people commit their talents to it (Laudin 1996:19). Kuhn argues "not merely that certain decisions between theories in science *have been irrational*, but that choices between competing scientific theories, in the nature of the case, *must be irrational*" (Laudin 1977:3; emphasis in the original). They all argue the impotence of positive instances to prove a theory, or of negative ones to disprove it, and that choices between paradigms are based on political and social factors such as prestige, power, and age rather than rational or empirical proofs of superiority. Consequently, scientific theories are neither true, nor probable, nor progressive, nor highly confirmed. Nor is there progress in scientific thought.

In the end, instrumentalism abandons all claims to truth. If we cannot judge between belief systems, all we have left is phenomenology—our attempts to describe and understand reality from our own perspective. Moreover, we cannot move beyond phenomenology—beyond describing as accurately as possible what we perceive to be reality. For instance, in studying other religions, we can, at best, describe what we understand of their beliefs. We cannot judge them to be true or false.

What of those who "convert" from one theory to another? Kuhn insists that scientists change theories not on the basis of reason but of subjective preference, as a "conversion experience," a "leap of faith," or a "Gestalt shift." Moreover, those who "go native" with respect to a new theory cannot explain it to their former colleagues. Each community, and ultimately each person, is imprisoned inside its own subjective worlds. The result is egocentrism and narcissism.

Incommensurability also means that ideas expressed in one language and culture cannot be accurately translated into other languages and cultures. As we will see, this has profound implications for translating the Bible into other languages.

If we cannot test for truth, on what basis can we judge between scientific theories? The answer is pragmatism—the "useful fictions"[5] that are good if they are useful and if they work. The purpose of science, therefore, is not to find truth about the external world but to control it for our own purposes. William James, an avowed pragmatist, wrote:

> *"The truth"... is only the expedient in the way of our thinking, just as "the right" is only the expedient in the way of our behaving.* Expedient is almost any fashion;... for what meets expediently all the experiences in sight won't necessarily meet all further experiences equally satisfactorily.... *The truth is the name of whatever proves itself to be good in the way of belief* (1946:22, 75–76; emphasis in the original).[6]

Instrumentalism begins by denying our ability to know truth. It ends in philosophical relativism. It rejects the view that "theories can be objectively compared, that theories are ever decisively refuted, that there are epistemically robust rules for theory selection that guide scientific choices, and that scientists holding different theories are fully capable of communicating with one another" (Laudin 1996:4–5). Postpositivists are thoroughgoing relativists because they are committed to the following views:

> (1) that evidence radically underdetermines theory choice—to the extent that virtually any theory can be rationally retained in the face of any conceivable evidence (epistemic relativism); (2) that the standards for theory evaluation are mere conventions, reflecting no facts of the matter (metamethodological relativism); and (3) that one conceptual framework or worldview cannot be made intelligible in the language of a rival (linguistic relativism) (Laudin 1996:5).

Dialogical Communities

If positivists locate authority in the individual, instrumentalists place it in the community of scholars who share a common paradigm. There is no private knowledge, no community-free ideas. It is the community that determines for itself the criteria of truth, formulates theories, and verifies them.

In such a setting, dialogue within a community is the path to knowledge. This is not a search to test theories against "reality." Rather, it is a Hegelian dialectic by which members seek to reach a consensus. Dialogue with other communities, too, is not to test whose paradigm is closer to the truth, but to understand and learn from one another and to find a common ground of agreement.

Disagreements

In instrumentalism, disagreements between people in and between paradigms cause no serious conflicts. A diversity of opinions on any subject is readily tolerated. Willard Oxtoby writes:

> The phenomenologist is obliged simply to set forth his understanding, as a whole, trusting that his reader will enter into it. There is no procedure stated by which he can compel a second phenomenologist to agree with the adequacy and incontrovertibility of his analysis, unless the second phenomenologist's "eidetic vision" [which suspends objectivity] happens to be same as the first's…. [T]here are as many phenomenologies as there are phenomenologists (1968:597–98).

Because no one claims to know the truth and because there are no objective criteria on which decisions can be made, disagreements do not drive the participants to reexamine their positions seriously.

The Characteristics of Idealism

A second response to the collapse of positivism has been a return to idealism. Because it is less present in scientific thought, I will examine it only briefly. Interestingly, the line between instrumentalism and idealism is a fine one. Both place knowledge firmly in the mind and do not derive it from external realities. The only certain reality we know is our ideas. Both recognize that as humans we can think only in terms of our own particular systems of knowledge, which are shaped by our historical and cultural contexts.

The difference between them has to do with the claims they make for knowledge. Instrumentalism ontologically assumes a real external world and sees knowledge as a "useful fiction" about that world. Idealism says that our knowledge itself is what is really real; the external world is a creation of our minds. Arnold Hauser notes, "The whole of empirical reality is only the image of a world of ideas" (Firth 1973:31). Consequently, idealism can strongly affirm its ideas as truth because only ideas are real.[7] Their difference is reflected in their responses to disagreements. In instrumentalism, arguments are no threat to the mental foundations of either party, for both recognize the subjective and tentative nature of knowledge. In idealism they lead to conflict or to isolationism, for each party claims to know the truth.

Subjectivism, Hermeneutics, and Dialogue

In idealism, knowledge is shaped in human minds by historical and cultural contexts. There is no privileged position from which objective truth can be examined, no real-word referent to which language is cemented. Ronald Sukenick notes:

> All versions of "reality" are of the nature of fiction. There's your story and my story, there's the journalist's story and the historian's story, there's the philosopher's story and the scientist's story... Our common world is only a description... reality is imagined (1976:113).

The task of science then is not to discover reality but to create it. Jean-François Lyotard writes: "It must be clear that it is our business not to supply reality but to invent allusions to the conceivable which cannot be presented" (1984:159).

In idealism, language itself is the only reality we know; consequently, reality is, at most, a linguistic habit. Everything is seen as "text," and meaning lies in the mind of the reader. These texts are thought to have no clear objective content. Consequently, readers are free to interpret the texts as they wish, using their emotions, intuitions, and imaginations. There is no way to test whether their interpretations are correct or whether anyone's is. There is little faith in reason, and a rejection of conventional criteria for evaluating knowledge objectively. Human discourse then becomes a power game with verbal negotiation, pressure, and lobbying designed to gain support, to "enroll," and to mobilize resources in order to gain an intellectual monopoly for the product.

Because radical idealism holds that all we have is ideas in people's heads, its basic task is hermeneutics—to seek to understand what is going on in the heads of others, or, indeed, of one's own. It replaces objective truth with hermeneutic truth that respects the subjectivity both of the speaker and the listener. In the end, we must even doubt our own subjectivity, for this is imposed on us in self-contradictory cultural packages. The hermeneutical method requires a Hegelian type of dialogue that seeks synthesis, not a joint search for the truth.

Disagreements

Because knowledge in idealism is created by the mind, we cannot resolve disagreements by appealing to empirical observations. Rather, they lead to conflicts of claims and counterclaims, and to fission. In fact, there is no common language people in different paradigms can use to talk to one another. They may use the same words, but because these are used with different meanings in different paradigms, there is no true understanding of one another.

Unity within a paradigm is maintained as disciples remain faithful to their guru or leader, or maintain a strong community consensus. The latter can be achieved, in part, by rejecting challenges to their fundamental assumptions as irrational and false, and by casting out those who disagree with them as heretics. The result, for those in a given paradigm, is a sense of unquestioned certainty about the knowledge they have.

Instrumentalism and Anthropology

Early anthropology looked at other people as objects to be studied by means of Western categories, logic and scientific methods. As anthropologists studied other peoples, however, they became increasingly conscious that these others were not primitive but fully rational beings with their own autonomous societies and cultures, and their own views of reality. It became clear that to use Western civilization as the standard to measure other peoples is ethnocentric to the core. Western cultures must be understood as a few among many. This awareness led to an epistemological shift in anthropology from positivism to instrumentalism—from ontology to phenomenology.

Two major streams of anthropological theory emerged after 1930. The British Structural Functionalists followed the lead of Durkheim and focused their studies on social systems. They saw each society as a unique, sui generis, organic whole. Each is discrete, bounded, and self-contained. Like a human body, each is made up of parts that "function" to maintain a harmonious, balanced whole. Changes, like diseases, are destructive.

A. R. Radcliffe-Brown, one of the early leaders in this school, held that people's behavior can best be explained by social facts and forces, not by their religious beliefs, which he saw as fictions created by societies to keep their people in line. Although he sought to understand the people's social organization from their point of view, his analysis was essentially etic in character. Bronislaw Malinowski, another of the early leaders, gave greater credence to beliefs in other societies. He argued that to understand Others we must enter their world, and see it in terms of their categories and logic— emically. The anthropologist must be a participant-as-observer, an insider-outsider, a scientist-native, an observer who knows the native language but speaks in English. In the process, Malinowski moved a long way toward an instrumentalist epistemology.

The American Historicists focused their studies on culture and cultural systems. They realized that the word "civilization" was arrogant and colonial, so they introduced the word "culture." Bernard McGrane writes:

> The emergence of the concept "culture" has made possible the democratization of differences.... The twentieth-century concept of "culture" has rescued the non-European Other from the depths of the past and prehistory and reasserted him in the present; he is, once again, contemporary with us. Twentieth-century "culture" was a concept forged in the teeth of "evolution," in a struggle to the death with "evolution" and the hierarchical scheme implicit in it (1989:114).

Anthropologists generally use "culture" in its plural form to affirm not only the autonomy of each culture but also the diversity of the cultures. Cultures in this school of thought are seen as morally neutral. There are no cultural universals by which they could be evaluated. Consequently, for people in one culture to judge those in another is condemned as ethnocentric and imperial.

At first, cultural anthropologists gave detailed etic descriptions of other cultures, but in time the shift has been to emic, or insider, views. This was first seen in the area of descriptive linguistics that emerged as a new field in anthropology. Later it led to New Anthropology, with its emphasis on ethno-musicology, ethno-psychology, ethno-methodology, and ethno-science. In each of these disciplines, external or etic frames of reference are rejected as intrinsically colonial. Anthropologists are to describe other cultures and worldviews using native categories and logic. At first this led to relativism as a research strategy, but eventually it led to the epistemological conclusion that all cultures are indeed autonomous paradigms, and relative to one another (Herskovits 1972). Edward Hall concludes that humans must "accept the fact that there are many roads to truth and no culture has a corner on the path or is better equipped than others to search for it. What is more, no man can tell another how to conduct that search" (1977:7).

Idealism has found little room in the sciences, but some anthropologists now argue that the ethnographic reports written by anthropologists tell us little about the people they studied, but are records of what happens in the minds of the anthropologists during their stay in the field. Some even argue that we can never really know anything, not even our own emotions (Schwartz 1990:32).

Instrumentalism, Idealism, and Postmodernism

Postmodernism is built on instrumentalist and idealist epistemologies. The term "postmodern" was used by a number of writers in the 1950s and 1960s, but the concept of postmodernism crystallized after the mid-1970s, when claims for its existence began to harden in and across a number of different academic disciplines.[8] Since the appearance of Jean-François Lyotard's *La Condition Postmoderne* in 1979, and its translation into English in 1984, it was clear that postmodernism and postmodernity could no longer be ignored.

Pauline Rosenau (1992:14–17) differentiates between two types of postmodernists—affirmative and skeptical. The former, she notes, sees hope that human thought, including the sciences, can provide answers to the many problems facing humankind. Skeptical postmodernists, on the other hand, see modern knowledge systems as the basis for the present crises and believe they must be rejected totally and replaced with another way of knowing. The former seem to use an instrumentalist epistemology for the most part, and the latter seem to be more idealists.

The relationship between modernity and postmodernity is a matter of considerable debate. Lyotard, Foucault, and others argue that postmodernity is a new era emerging out of the collapse of modernity. Richard Boyd (1984), Laudin (1996), and others argue that postpositivism (scientific instrumentalism) is positivism carried to its logical end—that postmodernity is modernity gone to seed. Like positivism, postpositivism is based on Cartesian skepticism and on the search for some sort of algorithm—mechanical in application—that can prove that one theory is better and more true than another. Positivists hoped, by these means, to prove scientific theories to be true. Postpositivists found that by these means no theory could be empirically and rationally determined. Harvey (1990) holds that postmodernity is, indeed, late modernity, but that it is sufficiently different to warrant a new label. Underlying the shift, he sees a shift from a system of capitalism based on the bureaucratic, centralized factories patterned after those built by Ford[9] to the new decentralized, flexible markets and modes of production. Behind these debates there is a broad consensus of what, in fact, are the characteristics of postmodernity. We need to examine these in more detail.

Subjectivism and Antimodernism

Many leading postmodernists call the whole enlightenment agenda into question. They argue that all knowledge is subjective and dependent on the context. K. Gergen notes (1986:141): "To the extent that the mind furnishes the categories of understanding, there are no real world objects to study other than those inherent within the mental makeup of persons." We have nothing but our mind games, and these are meaningless play.

Unrestricted by historic ties to empiricism, radical postmodern philosophy takes subjectivism to its logical limits. In its extreme forms it is antimodern, rejects epistemological assumptions, refutes methodological conventions, resists knowledge claims, obscures all version of truth, and dismisses policy recommendations (Rosenau 1992:3). It rejects the superiority of the present over the past, sees science as myth, and the Enlightenment heritage as totalitarian and culturally imperialistic. It gives priority to emotions, intuition, personal experience, the particular, and mystical experience. Ultimately, its goal is not to formulate an alternative set of assumptions but to register the impossibility of establishing any such underpinning for knowledge (Ashley and Walker 1990:264).

Experientialism and Existentialism

Postmodernity focuses on the self and the now—on the concrete in the form of daily life as an alternative to theory. It stresses appearance and image over technical and substance; the unique rather than the general; the unrepeatable rather than the reccurring; indeterminacy rather than determinism; diversity rather than unity; difference rather than synthesis. It is interested in the eccentric, the marginal, the disqualified, and the subjugated.

Postmodernity is deeply suspicious of reason. It sees reason as the basis of the Enlightenment, modernity, and Western society, and of their domination, oppression, and rule of the world. It therefore rejects reason as the basis for diversity and tolerance. "Abandoning reason means, for post-modernists, liberation from modernity's preoccupation with authority, efficiency, hierarchy, power, technology, commerce (the business ethic), administration and social engineering" (Rosenau 1992:129). Postmodernists celebrate emotions, intuition, creativity, and imagination. They accuse modernists of favoring

> the head over the heart; the mechanical over the spiritual or the natural...; the inertly impersonal over the richly personal...; the banal collective over the uniquely individual,... the dead tradition over the living experiment; the positivist experiment over the living tradition; the static product over the dynamic process;... dull sterile order over dynamic disorder;... the forces of death over the forces of life (Graff 1979:25).

Because of its stress on the present, postmodernism has little sense of history. Time is seen as disparate, crisscrossed, and misaligned rather than homogeneous, evolutionary, and purposive. It is fascinated with immediate events—with news.

Pluralism, Deconstructionism, and Relativism

Modernity has given rise to exploration, colonial expansion, global trade, and mass immigrations of people from one part

of the world to another. The result has been a growing awareness of cultural and religious pluralism. No longer are people
limited to certain territories. They are now found in great
diversity in every city around the world.

Day-to-day encounters with other kinds of people raise
the question of "otherness." How can people of different cultures and religions live together? The modern answer is that
all people are free, within very wide limits, to seek their own
home and to adopt and hold their own views, within the private sphere of life, of what is good and desirable. All of them,
however, must live under the hegemony of modernity, held
together by science, rational government and a common
economy.

The growing presence in the West of Indians, Koreans,
Africans, and Chinese, of Hindus, Muslims, and Buddhists
has begun to challenge this hegemony. They all claim the
right to keep their cultures and religions. The postmodern
answer to this growing pluralism is that different kinds of
people must learn to live together: each community lives in
its own enclave preserving its own distinctives, and each
must tolerate the differences of the others. The rival truth
claims of different cultures and religions must not lead to
argument. They must simply be accepted as part of a single
mosaic. The cardinal postmodern sins are ethnocentrism
and attempts to convert others to one's own beliefs and practices, or to control them.

Pluralism in everyday life is an increasing reality in the
lives of most ordinary people. The result is a growing state
of doubt about the nature of themselves and the universe in
which they live. The awareness of pluralism and relativity,
which has been shared by small groups of intellectuals, today
appears as a broad cultural fact reaching down into the ranks
of common folk.

One consequence of this pluralism is the loss of a single,
comprehensive worldview. Anthony Giddens notes:

> The condition of post-modernity is distinguished by an
> evaporating of the "grand narrative"—the overarching

"story line" by means of which we are placed in history as beings having a definite past and a predictable future. The post-modern outlook sees a plurality of heterogeneous claims to knowledge, in which science does not have a privileged place (1990:2).

Many postmodernists see the Grand Unified Theories of modernity and the hierarchies inherent in dichotomies like objective/subjective, right/wrong, good/bad, and pragmatic/principled as forms of intellectual tyranny. They argue that the only way to destroy this tyranny is to deconstruct the underlying intellectual systems and the social systems that sustain them.

Deconstructionists, such as Jacques Derrida, deny any coherent unity or logic to any text. They challenge the communicative power of language itself and seek to "decenter" its underlying structure and meaning.[10] They seek to demystify language by tearing it apart to reveal its internal, arbitrary hierarchies, flaws, and blindness. In doing so, they present as many interpretations as possible without affirming one over the other. David Harvey writes:

> I begin with what appears to be the most startling fact about postmodernism: its total acceptance of the ephemerality, fragmentation, discontinuity, and the chaotic.... But postmodernism... does not try to transcend it, contradict it, or even to define the "eternal and immutable" elements that might lie within it. Postmodernism swims, even wallows, in the fragmentary and the chaotic currents of change as if that is all there is... therefore, postmodernism typically harks back to that wing of thought, Nietzsche in particular, that emphasizes the deep chaos of modern life and its intractability before rational thought (1990:44).

Because neither theories nor knowledge systems make truth claims, there is no need to integrate them into a single grand conceptual scheme. Mutually contradictory theories and knowledge systems can be used. The collage, which creates ephemeral portraits by superimposing images to collapse a sense of time and space and accentuate the particular and personal, is the hallmark of postmodernity. One casualty of this deconstructionism is faith in humanly engineered progress.

Most postmodernists hold that all knowledge is context bound, and, therefore, relative to the knower and his or her context. Gellner points out:

> Relativism assumes or postulates a symmetrical world. Culture A has its own vision of itself and of culture B, and, likewise, B has its own vision of itself and of A. The same goes for the entire range of cultures. A must not sit in judgment on B nor vice versa, nor must B see A in terms of itself. Each must learn to see the other in terms of the other's own notions (if at all), and this is, presumably, the task and achievement of the hermeneutic anthropologist (1992:56).

Strange as it sounds, given its deconstruction of systems of knowledge, postmodernity seeks a comprehensive approach to knowledge. This does not mean that it is searching for a new integrated theory of knowledge. Rather, it means that all dimensions of human experience must be incorporated into the process of knowing: ideas, feelings, values, intuitions, and altered states of consciousness. Moreover, the perceptions of all points of view must be included and respected: Sioux, Cherokee, settler, rich, poor, feminine, masculine, Hindu, Muslim, aged, young, ad infinitum.

Instrumentalism, Idealism, and Christianity

What impact have instrumentalism and idealism had on Christianity and missions? Many of the current debates, both in theology and in mission, seem to reflect epistemological differences rather than disagreements over theological content. The results can be disconcerting. We use the same words, but we have the uneasy feeling that we are not all using them in the same ways.

Instrumentalism, Idealism, and Theology

The current crisis in epistemology has far-reaching consequences for theology. Forced to leave the comfort of a real world and certain knowledge, some theologians have chosen instrumentalism and its affirmation of a real world, and others have chosen idealism and its quest for mental certainty.

Instrumentalism and Theology

Postmodern theologians and scholars of religion are persuaded that all human knowledge is shaped by cultural and historical contexts. If this is true, then theology, too, is influenced by the culture and historical experiences of the theologians. There can be no totally objective theology. It is our human search for God—our God-talk, not God's revelation to us. This means that we must speak of "theologies," not Theology, for there are as many theologies as there are human points of view. There are African, Indian, and Chinese theologies; feminine and masculine theologies; and theologies of the oppressed, the powerful, and the middle class.

This pluralism calls for a radically different view of theology. David Tracy redefines it as "philosophical reflection upon the meanings present in common human experience and language, and upon the meanings present in the Christian fact" (1979:43). In other words, theology must emerge out of human historical and sociocultural contexts, and out of felt human needs, not out of a study of Scripture. Salvation is defined as liberation and dignity now, not some ultimate deliverance. Consequently, a great emphasis is placed on personal experience. Schleiermacher, for example, argued that reality lies in the believing soul, not in historical fact. He wrote: "As often as I turn my gaze inward upon my inmost self, I am at once within the domain of eternity" (Mackintos 1964:65). He comes to the fact of God by inference from his feeling of dependence. Doctrines of God are not statements about God himself but descriptions of our own feelings toward him. This emphasis on subjective experience is accompanied by a distrust of unified theologies that are seen as arid, dead, and oppressive, imposed on others by experts. Christianity becomes an intensely personal concern expressed in a closed community of faith.

More recently, attention has been turned to the proliferation of theologies as Christians in different cultures do theology in their own cultural and historical contexts. We now speak of African Theology, Asian Theology, and Latin American Theology. The result is a global crisis of meaning and truth. Is theology nothing more than the projections of our images of God? As we will see later, the crisis of theological pluralism is accentuated by debates over religious pluralism.

Instrumentalism has helped us challenge the ahistorical and acultural nature of positivist theology, and has reminded us that all human knowledge is shaped in the context of particular cultural and historical settings. And it has forced us to examine more deeply the relationship between human knowledge and reality. In so doing, it challenges the arrogance and ethnocentrism of Western thought. It also reminds us that theology must be the task of a community of faith and must touch human lives at the point of their felt needs.

But the weaknesses of instrumentalist theologies outweigh their strengths. Theology is reduced to our human search for God. The fact that divine revelation given to us in the Scriptures gives us a view of reality from outside our subjective human systems—a view that we can understand as objective truth—is denied. All we have is subjective theologies, not Theology. The result is theological relativism that denies any claim to truth, and ecclesiological fragmentation that separates Christians into incommensurable theological communities.

Idealism and Theology

Having to choose between certain human knowledge and the reality of the external world, some Christians have opted for some form of idealism with its theological certainty.[11] In this, human knowledge is seen as true in every detail, and experiences as contingent. Islamic, Hindu, and other fundamentalisms today are examples of such idealist reactions to science and modernity. They seek to counter the empiricism, secularism, and amorality of Western societies by a dogmatic affirmation of their own principal beliefs.

Christian idealists argue that we can have certainty in a theology that rests on Scripture and is unaffected by the historical and cultural contexts of the theologian. An idealist approach to theology does provide a viable way of looking at reality; there are too many idealists in philosophy and theology to write idealism off lightly. But it leaves us with difficult problems when it comes to Scriptures, Bible translation, missions, and cross-cultural communication. Scripture itself is a historical document, recorded in other cultures and times, and read by us today in our contexts. This raises again the problems of hermeneutics and subjectivity. In the end, idealists must appeal to human reason as the final arbiter of truth.

Idealist theologies seek to preserve the certainty of objective truth and absolutes. They reject the relativism that leads us to nihilism, but the price of this certainty is high. To claim that what is in the mind is objective reality is to deny the ultimate reality of God and his deeds in history. It is to locate truth in the self and to deify the human mind. And, as many Third World theologians point out, it can lead to Western theological colonialism and a failure to take them seriously.

Theology and Science

There is little conflict between science and theology in an instrumentalist epistemology. Science and theology are seen not as different kinds of knowing, but as pragmatic solutions to different human problems. Both must be measured by their results. But this undervalues both science and theology. Few scientists would agree that astronomy is no closer to the truth than astrology. Most are convinced that they are discovering truth about nature. Similarly, no evangelical would hold a relativistic view of theology that affirms that Christ is not the truth, not even a truth, but only a useful idea that helps us live better lives.

In an idealist mode, science and religion must be integrated into a single ideological system. Ultimately, the distinction

between them must be broken down. So, too, must the distinctions between spirit and matter, and idea and reality.
Often idealist systems of knowledge reduce the diversity of
human experience to monism or pantheism.[12]

Instrumentalism and Missions

An instrumentalist epistemology changes our view of
Christian mission. Because all religions are seen as
autonomous, incommensurable paradigms, and because we
have no privileged position from which to judge them, we
must affirm them as subjectively true. This undermines the
very essence of mission. Similarly, all cultures are seen as
good, and their preservation with minimal change an
unquestioned good. Lamin Sanneh calls this "cultural fundamentalism" (1993:29).

Evangelism and Mission

From an instrumentalist perspective, it is clear that the task
of missions is not to evangelize and seek to win people from
other religions to follow Jesus Christ. All religions must be
respected as a people's way of seeking God. Dialogue in the
Hegelian sense, not the proclamation of the Christian gospel,
is the basis of Christian missions. Our task is to join people
in other religions in their search for dignity and freedom, and
to learn from them what we find helpful for ourselves.
Mission is mission to us rather than to the people we serve.

Mission is also ministry to people according to their felt
needs. We must begin where people are and let them define
the agenda and the solutions. We must focus on this world
and the present. Salvation is defined as justice and liberation
from oppressive systems, as living together in harmony in a
pluralistic world, and as dignity experienced through leading
meaningful lives on earth. Our task is to join in solidarity
with those who are suffering from oppression and dehuman-
izing social systems by identifying ourselves with their pain.

Bible Translation and Contextualization

Instrumentalism and Saussurian linguistics, with their separation between form and meaning, have had a significant

impact on Bible translation. No longer are literal word-for-word translations seen as ways to preserve the accuracy of biblical ideas in other languages. The task of translators is to convey as much as possible the dynamic equivalents—the spirit, impact, and meanings the Scriptures had in their time—in new linguistic and cultural contexts.[13] What is important, therefore, are the meanings and responses that the translation generates in the minds of the readers. In translating between different languages, however, it is often necessary to change linguistic forms in order to preserve their meaning. For example, in societies where there is no "snow," the translator may use "milk" to preserve the sense of "whiteness" implicit in the passage (Isa. 1:18). Similarly, the statement that "a man who has put his hand to the plow should not look back [or he will plow a crooked furrow]" (Luke 9:62) can be translated among the Wanana of Panama, who have no agriculture, as "a man who has put his hand to the pole [to push the canoe up river] should not look back [for it will cause him to overturn the boat]."

This separation of form and meaning allows us to be more creative when we seek to translate and contextualize the gospel, but it raises the question whether such translations are accurate. Moreover, what do we mean by accurate? If meanings are arbitrarily linked to forms, new meanings can be given to old forms, and the same meaning can take on several different forms. The problem is, with no objective reality against which to test meaning, there is no way to test whether it is preserved in communication or through time. Pushed to the extreme, the purpose of Bible translation is not to preserve its meanings accurately but to stimulate responses in the minds of the readers. Communication then must focus on receptor-oriented communication. The listeners rule, for they are free to interpret the message as they wish.

The separation of form and meaning in symbols leads us to radical approaches to contextualization. Old cultural forms can be preserved so long as they are given new meanings. Because meanings are not found in symbols and acts, but in people's heads, what we need is mental changes, not changes in forms and behavior. In the extreme, this means a

Muslim convert to Christianity can continue to go to the Mosque and bow toward Mecca so long as he mentally worships "Jesus" instead of "Muhammed." Conversion is to change one's inner realities. It does not call for radical changes in the lives of people or a break with their cultures.

Other Religions

Ultimately, instrumentalism leads us to religious relativism and to the denial of the uniqueness of Christ as the only way of salvation.[14] The stage for this was set by the birth of the new discipline of comparative religion, which deals with religious pluralism by seeing all religions as human creations, and subjects them to the same criteria in comparisons.[15] The first step was the emergence of an inclusive theology of religions that sought truths in other religions that agree with biblical revelation. For example, J. N. Farquhar argued that Christianity is the fulfillment of other religions (1971). Raimundo Panikkar goes further and affirms that there is a hidden Christ in all religions (1981) and that people can be saved in their traditional ways, at least until they hear the gospel of Jesus Christ. Interreligious dialogue, then, is to listen to the voice of Christ that mysteriously speaks to us through the voice of our non-Christian partners because he is already present in the depth of their souls.

A second step in relativizing all religions was the introduction of a pluralistic theology of religions. Here all religions are granted equal status on the assumption that they all strive for the salvation of humankind on earth (Hick 1987). Salvation here is defined as social liberation, ecological harmony, or the peaceful coexistence of all religious traditions. Paul Knitter (1985), for example, affirms that all religions are equally valid, he advocates not the integration of all religions in one world faith but a wider religious ecumenism in which each religious community affirms and lives in harmony with other communities. To find common grounds for discussions, we must move away from a Christocentric theology to a theocentric theology. Some go beyond this and argue that to include all humans, atheists as well, theology must deal with the central human problems of justice, peace, and the integrity of creation. In this setting, interreligious dialogue helps mutual understanding and enables people to find areas of agreement necessary for peaceful coexistence. Joint services are encouraged in which people of different religions participate in one another's acts of worship.

Given this affirmation of religious pluralism, it should not surprise us that evangelism and the missionary movement are widely condemned as imperialist and arrogant. No religion has a right to judge the others, and because Christianity is only one religion among many, it must not seek to make converts from the others. The goal in missions, in an instrumentalist epistemology, is dialogue—to attempt to understand and learn from those in other religions and to find some grounds for agreement. It is not to lead people to faith in Jesus Christ as the only way to salvation.

Idealism and Missions

Idealism shapes missions in other ways. First, it fosters a separation of the gospel from cultural contexts and seeks to define the gospel as pure and simple—in pure Platonic forms (Sanneh 1993:117). But this makes the gospel a pure abstraction, stripped of all cultural entanglements, divorced from the grimy realities of human life, and powerless in transforming real humans and their sociocultural systems. Second, because communication and understanding between ideological paradigms are impossible, comparison and testing are also impossible. Third, as we see in Muslim and Hindu fundamentalism, radical idealism often leads to a rigid dogmatism with regard to its own message, and to attacks on others as evil and pagan. It rejects dialogue and often appears to be arrogant. Idealism also rejects contextualization, for it affirms the truth of its own paradigm. The truth it affirms must be communicated in other cultures without change, because to translate or contextualize it is to distort it.[16]

Attacks on Instrumentalism

In recent years there have been growing challenges in academia to instrumentalism, idealism, and postmodernity

(Laudin 1996; Rosenau 1992). These have come from different directions.

One attack against total subjectivism comes from within semiotics. Many scholars now reject the belief that human symbols are arbitrary and that meaning lies only in the mind. For example, Brent Berlin and Paul Kay (1969) show that color categories in different languages are not arbitrary cultural creations but do correlate to external realities. Although they vary from culture to culture, these variations follow a certain order. By analyzing this order, Berlin and Kay formulate a theory that enables us to correlate color terms with light waves and sensory stimuli. This makes it is possible for us to compare and translate the denotative meanings of color terms from one culture to another. Eugene Hunn (1982) and Jay Miller (1982) have compared the taxonomies of birds and plants in different cultures, and find a high degree of agreement on the essentials. In other words, scientific theories are not simply "useful fictions."[17]

A second attack is leveled against the relativism of instrumentalism. On the cognitive level, instrumentalism leaves us with no new foundations on which to build objective understandings of reality and truth. On the cultural level, it denies any common human understanding (cf. Hollis and Likes 1982; Jarvie 1984).[18] Marvin Harris writes:

> To deny the validity of etic [external scientific] descriptions is in effect to deny the possibility of a social science capable of explaining sociocultural similarities and differences. To urge that the etics of scientific observers is merely one among any infinity of other emics [unexamined cultural views]—the emics of Americans and Chinese, of women and men, of blacks and Puerto Ricans, of Jews and Hindus, of rich and poor, and of young and old—is to urge the surrender of our intellects to the supreme mystification of total relativism (1980:45).

On the moral front, relativism requires a rejection of all ideas of good and evil. But, as Peter Berger notes, some acts, such as the Nazi gas chambers, are so evil that to refuse to condemn them in absolute terms would offer prima facie evidence "not only of a profound failure in the understanding of judgment, but more profoundly of a fatal impairment of *humanitas*" (1970:66). Harris is even more vehement in his attack.

> The doctrine that all fact is fiction and that all fiction is fact is a morally depraved doctrine. It is a doctrine that conflates the attacked with the attacker; the tortured with the torturer; and the killed with the killer. It is true that at Dachau there was the SS' story; and the prisoners' story;... and that at Kent State there was the guardsmen's story and the story of the students shot in the back, five hundred feet away. Only a moral cretin would wish to maintain that all these stories could be equally true (1980:324).

Gellner adds:

> Relativism does entail nihilism: if standards are inherently and inescapably expressions of something called culture, and can be nothing else, then no culture can be subjected to a standard, because (*ex hypothesi*) there cannot be a transcultural standard which would stand in judgement over it (1992:50).

A third attack against instrumentalism has to do with its logical inconsistencies. As Fuller points out, a person cannot participate in the debate on scientific realism—even as an instrumentalist—unless he or she is a historical realist and believes that historical inquiry is as epistemologically sound as any other empirical inquiry (1991:65). Moreover, relativism relativizes all other views but absolutizes its own.

Finally, postmodernity, the offspring of instrumentalism and idealism, has no agenda of its own to solve the world's problems. It is reactive, not proactive, and its fundamental agenda is to oppose modernity and its fruits. As Rosenau points out, it is a luxury for those who have plenty. Little attention is paid to it in Eastern Europe, China, or the rest of the world (1992:11). Laudin, a student of Kuhn, is particularly caustic in his evaluation of postpositivism or instrumentalism.

> In my view, postpositivism is an intellectual failure. The arguments on its behalf are dubious and question-begging. Still worse, it has sustained virtually no positive program of research... And if that is correct, then it is time to start over again in philosophy of science, distancing ourselves as far as we possibly can from some of the pervasive assumptions... that... turn out to be the undoing of positivism and postpositivism alike (1996:6).

Ultimately, instrumentalism and radical idealism collapse under the weight of their own internal contradictions. Both use reason to discredit rationality. Both absolutize relativism. But, as Berger writes, we may need to go through the relativizing of all human cultures before we can come out on the other side on more firm ground.

> [Relativism] pushed to its final consequence bends back upon itself. The relativizers are relativized, the debunkers are debunked—indeed, relativization itself is somehow liquidated. What follows is not, as some of the early sociologists of knowledge feared, a total paralysis of thought. Rather it is a new freedom and flexibility in asking questions of truth.... Once we know that all human affirmations are subject to scientifically graspable socio-historical processes, *which affirmations are true and which are false?* We cannot avoid the question any more than we can return to the innocence of its pre-relativizing asking. This loss of innocence, however, makes for the difference between asking the question before and after we have passed through the "fiery brook" (1970:40, 42; emphasis in the original).

Although Berger, Laudin, and other critics of postmodernity may be correct about its state in the academic community, postmodernity continues to spread as an increasingly powerful force in Western societies. Modern nations struggle to integrate different peoples and religions within the same state, and global businesses must deal with cultural differences. Local communities must deal with racism, hatred, and violence that are endemic to pluralistic societies. Postmodernity in public life is by no means dead.

Churches in the West, too, have not adequately come to grips with the problems raised by cultural and religious pluralism. Most congregations remain segregated, and racism is not strongly addressed. Most Western Christians have yet to develop epistemological foundations that enable them to affirm the uniqueness of Christ as the only way to salvation and life eternal, and to witness boldly to the truth in winsome ways. Formerly, missionaries faced the questions raised by religious pluralism. Today, Western Christians ride to work with Muslims and Hindus who are good people, often better than some Christians they know. How can they declare that these people are lost? The easy solution is to stress tolerance, to live our own lives and let others live theirs, and to hope that communities can somehow coexist in peace in the same nation and world. One of the greatest challenges to the Western church is to lay again the theological foundations of the truth of the gospel and to train its members how to proclaim this with humility and love.

3

Critical Realism—A Way Ahead

In the past, positivism provided what appeared to be firm epistemic foundations for science, but instrumentalism destroyed them, leaving science in a vortex of relativism. What lies ahead? Peter Berger likens the epistemological scene to people walking confidently along on solid ground until they come to a river. Wanting to continue on, they wade into the water. At first the venture is interesting, but as the water reaches their necks, some turn back trying to regain the firm ground of positivism they have left. Others continue and are swept away by the stream of relativism when their feet no longer touch bottom. Still others swim on and come to the firm ground of critical realism on the other side, and move on. What is this "ground" ahead?

Critical Realism and Science

Instrumentalism and postmodernism are valid reactions to the arrogance of positivism, with its sense of intellectual superiority and rejection of the knowledge of other cultures; but the cure is worse than the disease. They have no truth to affirm and no agenda to solve the growing problems on earth. They are "post" this, and "anti" that.

In recent years there has been a growing interest in critical realism as an alternative to the positivism of modernity and the instrumentalism/idealism of postmodernity.[1] Most scientists are not interested in questions of epistemology; they carry on their work convinced that they are in search of truth and that their theories are more than useful fictions (Laudin 1996:149). With the exception of some social scientists, few are idealists, and with the exception of some applied and social scientists, few are instrumentalists. In this setting, critical realism offers an alternative that is more humble but also more proactive in its response to the human dilemma. If postmodernity is linked to instrumentalism and idealism, then we might argue that critical realism is associated with the new emerging globalism.

The Nature of Critical Realism

Critical realist epistemology strikes a middle ground between positivism, with its emphasis on objective truth, and instrumentalism, with its stress on the subjective nature of human knowledge (Figure 7). It affirms the presence of objective truth but recognizes that this is subjectively apprehended. On another level, as Laudin points out (1996), it challenges the definition of "rationality" in both positivism and instrumentalism that limits rationality to algorithmic logic. In so doing, critical realism offers a third, far more nuanced, epistemic position.

Critical Realism

Critical realism, or "critical common-sensism" as Charles Peirce called it, is both "realistic" and "critical." Ontologically, it is a form of realism, for it assumes a real world that exists independently from human perceptions or opinions of it. It is critical, for it examines the processes by which humans acquire knowledge and finds that this knowledge does not have a literal one-to-one correspondence to reality. Peirce, one of the fathers of critical realism, argues:

> There are Real things, whose characters are entirely independent of our opinions about them; those Reals affect our senses according to regular laws, and, though our sensations are as different as are our relations to the objects, by taking advantage of the laws of perception,

Characteristics of Epistemological Positions

Idealism	Mentalism (reality is in the mind) - knowledge is itself the object of analysis - we know it with certainty	Dogmatic (closed to change) - knowledge is exact and cumulative - declarative in stance - ahistorical and acultural in nature - authoritarian - parent/child approach to others - learning = memorizing - teacher and message oriented - at times arrogant and combative - conversion is radical displacement	Absolutes (affirms that truth can be known) - can know in full - can know in full - knowledge is totally objective	Choice (humans reason and choose)
Naive Realism	Realism (reality is the world including the mind. Tests knowledge against experience and history) - knowledge is totally objective - photograph view of knowledge			
Critical Realism	- knowledge is both subjective and objective - map or model view of knowlege	Affirmational (open to change) - testimonial and irenic in nature - sees knowledge in cultural and historical contexts - adult/adult approach - concern for person and messge - learner oriented - teach students to think - more humble attitude - conversion = a new gestalt	- know only in part - knowledge is both objective and subjective	
Instrumentalism	- knowledge is totally subjective		Relativism (denies that truth can be known) - pragmatism - test its usefulness: does it work? - anticonversion	
Determinism				Deterministic (no human reason or choice)

Figure 7

Source: Paul G. Hiebert. The missiological implications of an epistemological shift. *TSF Bulletin.* 8.5 (May–June 1985): p. 14. Used by permission.

we can ascertain by reasoning how things really and truly are; and any man, if he have sufficient experience and he reason enough about it, will be led to the one True conclusion (1955:18).

Like instrumentalism, critical realism distinguishes between reality and our knowledge of it; but like positivism, it claims that that knowledge can be true. Critical realism also assumes, ontologically, that the world is orderly and that that order can be comprehended, in some measure, by human reason. A chaotic and causeless universe that does not obey the principle of sufficient reason (things are the way they are for a reason and change only for a reason) cannot support an ordered science or religion.

Triadic Symbols

Peirce proposed a third way of looking at symbols, words, formulas, and other signs that mediate our perceptions of reality. He rejected the positivist equation of meaning and form, and the instrumentalist equation of meaning with mental images. Peirce argued that a sign has three parts to it (Figure 8): (1) an exterior form (the *signifier*; e.g., the spoken or written word, the sound of a bell, the shape of an arrow); (2) a mental concept or image (the *signification*); and (3) the reality the sign refers to (the *signified*). For example, the word "tree" invokes a mental image of a tree and refers to real trees in nature. A photograph is a picture of a real person that evokes images of that person in our mind when we see it, even though that person is not present. In other words, a sign links mental images to realities, real or imagined, by means of words, gestures, sounds, and other signifiers. If only two dimensions are present, it is not a true sign.

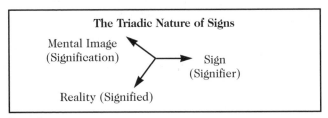

Figure 8

Signs link our mental world to the external world. They have a subjective dimension (the image in our mind), an objective dimension (the real trees to which we are referring), and a symbolic dimension (the sign, such as a word that is part of a sign system or language). Because of their objective dimension, it is possible, in many cases, to test whether our signs "fit" or "do not fit" the real world. This keeps signs from being purely arbitrary, culturally shaped categories. For instance, as children we learn the meaning of words from our experiences and our mistakes. Our mother points to a bird and says "duck," so we say "duck." She points to another and again says "duck." We parrot back "duck." Then we see a bird and say "duck," but mother corrects us and says "no, that's a goose." In time we learn to differentiate between ducks and geese, not by memorizing definitions in dictionaries but by learning from our experiences.

A triadic view of signs sees meaning not in objective realities or in subjective mental images. Rather, it is found in the *correspondence* between ideas and reality mediated through sign systems. Correspondence, here, may take different meanings. For example, in formal signs the relationship between the sign and reality is one of direct reference—of what we have called a "photograph" of reality. In metaphorical signs, as we will see later, the correspondence is more complex and includes the ideas of analogy and allegory. It is easy for us to create mental categories, but if these do not correspond in some way to anything real, they are often useless. On the other hand, it is hard for us to see things for which we have no categories. We use signs to refer mentally to realities, real or imagined, and we test our categories against these realities to determine their fit.

Signs are the building blocks that enable us to construct mental worlds of reality as we perceive it. We use these inner worlds to live in the external world and to manipulate it. In our minds we think of our house, and drive to it. We mentally picture a purple cow, so we paint our cow purple.

The objective-subjective nature of Peircian signs has far-reaching implications. It holds that all knowledge has both objective and subjective dimensions to it. Examining the objective dimensions of signs, Brent Berlin and Paul Kay (1969) found that color categories in different languages are culturally shaped, but not arbitrary.[2] Studying taxonomies of birds and plants, Eugene Hunn (1982) and Jay Miller (1982) have shown that some cultures lump together certain species that other cultures split, but that there is a basic agreement on the fundamental categories in nature. For example, no language lumps cows and birds into a single category, or goats with trees. The deep structures of linguistic categories, at least those dealing with the experiential world, reflect not only culturally determined divisions but also real divisions in the nature of reality itself. The meaning of concepts must be understood not only with regard to the set of cultural and semiotic connotations with which they are associated but also to the realities (signified) to which they refer.

On the other hand, signs have a subjective dimension to them. Von Weizscker writes: "We may speak of objects only in as much as they are possible objects of a subject. This sentence, too, is almost a truism since we define knowledge as the knowledge of an object by a subject" (Torrance 1978:95). Scientists such as Einstein, Polanyi, and von Weizscker have shown us that even physical scientists are part of the picture they observe. Scientific propositions are statements about what the scientist can observe and do as well as statements about nature itself. Scientific laws are expressions of the processes of human cognition and of the historical and cultural contexts of scientists, as well as of external realities themselves.

But this active involvement by the scientist in the formulation of knowledge raises the question of subjectivity. Does it not destroy the possibility of objectivity—of knowledge that is true, as instrumentalists argue? Werner Heisenberg contends otherwise. On the level of primary observation and the recording of empirical data, he writes:

> The introduction of the observer must not be misunderstood to imply that some kind of subjective features are to be brought into the description of nature.

> The observer has, rather, only the function of regis-
> tering decisions, i.e., processes in space and time, and
> it does not matter whether the observer is an appara-
> tus or a human being; but the registration, that is, the
> transition from the "possible" to the "actual," is
> absolutely necessary here and cannot be omitted from
> the interpretation of quantum theory (1962:137).

On higher levels of cognition, as we will see, critical realism
draws on community hermeneutics, metacultural grids, and a
broad range of rational analysis to test the validity of theories.

Critical realism does not claim pure objectivity for
human knowledge. In fact, it argues that total objectivity, if
that could be achieved, would not be knowledge, for knowledge is more than factual information. It is used by people to
live their lives. Knowledge in critical realism is the correspondence between our mental maps and the real world; it is
objective reality subjectively known and appropriated in
human lives.

Critical realism also restores emotions and moral judgments as essential parts of "knowing" and argues that these
do not necessarily negate the objectivity of scientific observations. As I. C. Jarvie points out (1984), to divorce morality
from rationality and knowledge is to destroy both. Knowledge
is not impersonal facts that can be stored in a computer as
well as in a head. It is ideas that interact with feelings and
values in complex ways to produce decisions and actions.
Polanyi points out that we are morally responsible for the
use of the knowledge we have. Knowledge itself is power,
and individuals and groups use and misuse it for their own
advantage.

Natural scientists observe mute objects, but social scientists study human "objects" who are thinking and responding
subjects in their own right. This adds a second type of subjective reality to the picture—the ideas, feelings, and values
internal to human beings being studied. These are no less
real than the material world, but their inclusion raises a
number of difficult issues.

The objective-subjective nature of knowledge provides us with an answer to the problem of learning to "know" another person. Positivists can make statements about the external characteristics of humans—their material beings and behavior—but not about their inner selves. Moreover, it often reduces them to mechanical objects. In critical realism we take the ideas, feelings, values, and purposes of people to be real, and seek to understand them as human beings as they reveal themselves to us. The fact that knowledge links inner worlds to outer realities makes such knowing possible. Interpersonal knowing is not simply knowledge about a person, but knowing the person intimately as fully human—as we know ourselves.

The study of interhuman communication involves hermeneutics—the processes by which we seek to know the inner world of another person (Osborne 1991). This is not a one-way activity. It involves a dialogue in which we both learn about others and reveal ourselves to them. The presence of scientists affects the people they study. People say and do things to impress or manipulate the scientist, and hide other things because they do not trust him or her. The task of interpersonal hermeneutics is a complex one, full of pitfalls.

Hermeneutics raises the question of two "realities." Both the scientists and the people they study have their own interpretations of the world. To differentiate between these two views, anthropologists have coined the terms *emic* and *etic*. Emic statements are the people's view of things. The test of the adequacy of an emic analysis is the ability of the scientist to generate statements the people accept as real, meaningful, and appropriate. In carrying out research in the emic mode, the observer attempts to acquire a knowledge of the categories, rules, and logic one must know in order to think and act as a native. Etic statements are the scientists' view of things. They involve the use of the categories and logic developed by science based on the analysis and comparison of many different cultures. The test of their adequacy is their ability to generate scientifically productive theories about human realities and the causes of sociocultural differences and similarities (Harris 1980:32).

The question arises, Whose explanation of reality is right? Is science closer to the truth than explanations offered in other cultures? Or are they all true? How can we test which system of explanation is more true? It is on this issue that the social sciences split between the instrumentalists who declare that all cultural explanations are equally valid, and the critical realist who holds that some systems of explanation can be shown to be better descriptions of reality than others. How can scientists (or theologians, or anyone) claim that some systems of knowledge are better (and what do we mean by "better") than others without returning to positivism and its arrogance? Are they not forever culture bound themselves? We will examine this later when we look at the question of truth.

The objective-subjective link also reintroduces teleology as a valid part of scientific analysis. In positivism, when we see a man going to a shop, we cannot explain his actions in terms of his intentions. We must limit our explanations to antecedent causes. In critical realism, we are free to use purpose as a valid explanation for human actions.

Finally, the introduction of scientists into the observed reality makes science reflexive. In passing theoretical judgments on the people they observe, scientists are passing judgments on themselves, for they, too, are humans. Scientific theories must apply equally to the scientists themselves as well as to the people they study. For example, behavioralism must make sense when applied not only to subjects under investigation but also to the scientists as they formulate their behavioralist theories.

Models, Maps, and Blueprints

Critical realism affirms that human knowledge does represent reality, but by "represent" it does not mean the formal or literal one-to-one correspondence of photographs. Rather, it sees knowledge as models, maps, or blueprints of reality. These may be "true," but in a certain way. The nature of representation and truth in critical realism can be seen by analyzing the relationship between a map and the reality it maps. In the first place, the correspondence between map and reality is symbolic and analogical.[3] A map is not a photograph of reality. It is a model, a mental diagram or schema, an analogical representation that conveys limited but accurate information about reality. It is a system of symbols that represent particular aspects of reality. This information has to do not only with the existence of entities but also with the relationships that exist between them (Figure 9).

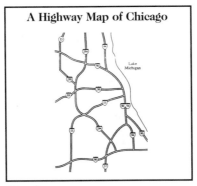

A Highway Map of Chicago

Figure 9

Unlike literal representations, maps have information that does not correspond literally with the external world. A schematic map, such as that of Chicago freeways, does not show every curve and bridge on the roads, nor are the lengths on the map proportionate to distances in reality. Such information poses no problem so long as we know that no correspondence is intended. We do not reject a map as false simply because every detail of reality is not included and accurately presented.

Meaning in maps is not the sum of bits of information and truth. It is in the configuration that orders bits of information into an interpretive whole. There are objective facts, but there are also our subjective interpretations of these facts. Let us return to our earlier example of ten dots. These are the "facts," but given our human need to give meaning to experience, we tend to see a star (Figure 10). The question is, Does the star exist in reality, or is it created by the mind of the beholder? The answer is both. The observer does add the interpretation that this has the shape of a star. Another observer might see two pentagons or two circles. On the other hand, the observer would not see a star if the dots were not placed in a way that can be interpreted as a star. If they were placed randomly on the page, we would not be led to order them as a star.

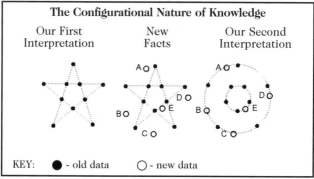

Figure 10

A second question arises, Which interpretation of the dots more closely fits the underlying order of the dots themselves? To answer this we need to look for more dots that will eliminate some interpretations and confirm other ones. For example, if further research shows us a dot at point A, we would begin to question our interpretation of the dots as a star. If further facts emerge at points B, C, and D, we would be forced to reject that understanding in favor of two circles.

It is the configurational nature of knowledge that gives meaning to uninterpreted experiences. It gives to knowledge a coherence and comprehension that makes sense out of a bewildering barrage of sense data entering our mind.

The configurational nature of knowledge is also important in understanding change in knowledge systems. Normal change occurs as new data are added and lines are redrawn here and there to fit the new information. Revolutions, or what Kuhn calls "paradigm shifts," occur when the existing configuration is rejected because it no longer adequately accounts for the data, and a new configuration is adopted that explains the data better. In Figure 10, this occurs when we suddenly realize that two circles better explain the new information than does a star. But total paradigm shifts at the macrolevel rarely, if ever, take place (Laudin 1996:89–97). Rather, changes generally occur as microparadigm shifts at the level of specific theories and parts of theories due to encounters with other theories.[4] Such changes do affect the overall configuration of the paradigm, but the paradigm as a whole is not displaced by another.

In positivism, conversion (or paradigm shifts) requires a rejection of all the elements of the old theory, for a theory is made up of the sum of its parts. To include an element from the old in the new is to contaminate it. In critical realism, elements of the old paradigm can be incorporated in the new, but because they are part of a new configuration, they take on new meanings. Furthermore, because meaning is found in the configuration, not every fact must be present, or even accurate, for us to see the larger pattern. Approximate data are often adequate for us to understand what is going on (Figure 11). These observations will be important when we consider conversion in Christian missions.

Picture of a Young Boy

[Note: Not every bit of information need to be present or accurate for us to grasp the picture.]

Figure 11

Maps illustrate other characteristics of analogical signs. First, they can speak of realities invisible to the human eye. Coloring one state red and the next yellow does not mean that they are, in fact, red and yellow. It does speak of political realities we cannot see driving along the freeway, but these political realities are very real. Which police have jurisdiction and what laws we must observe are determined by state and national boundaries that we cannot see. Similarly, we can map religious beliefs, linguistic boundaries, and wealth—none of which is readily visible to the naked eye.

Second, maps must be selective. No map can chart the real world in its entirety. If every street, driveway, and sidewalk; every pole and house; every telephone wire and underground pipe of a city are charted on one map, it becomes cluttered and useless. Every map purports to give us true information, but only about some part of reality. It may be a map of roads or of sewers, or of ethnic distributions in a city. It is this selectivity that determines for each map what is essential information that must be included on that map, and what is nonessential and can be dropped or stylized. The truthfulness of a map is not measured by the accuracy of its extraneous information but of the information it claims to present truthfully. One does not reject a road map because it does not include every bend and bridge. If we are going to the airport, it makes little difference to us whether the road crosses the stream here or there, so long as the road shown on the map gets us there.

Third, to be true, a map must have positive analogies—areas in which there is a direct correspondence with reality. If in the outside world freeway 90 is north of freeway 290, this must be symbolically represented on a road map. If the analogies a map claims to make are not true, the map is false. Many analogies have to do more with the relationship between things than with the intrinsic nature of things themselves. Maps also have neutral analogies—areas in which the correspondence to the world has not yet been explored. We know the road we are on is going east and postulate that it will come to the north-south highway, so we drive to see if it does. In doing so we fill in our mental map.

In this way maps are heuristic; they can always be improved and need continuous study. Much of scientific research is designed to "map" the unexplored areas of reality.

Finally, a map is purposive. As Clifford Geertz points out (1979), maps or models have two purposes. On the one hand, they are maps *of* reality. They help us understand the true nature of things. On the other hand, models are maps *for* action. We use them to guide our actions.

Does the fact that knowledge takes the form of models and maps mean that these are nothing more than logical fictions? Leonard Nash says a firm "no."

> We must not then take a theoretical model too literally; indeed *we may err by taking the model too literally.* But as we would realize the full heuristic power inherent in it, *we must take the model very seriously....* If our models are to lead us to ask, and seek answers for new questions about the world, we must regard them as something more than "logical superfluities," "illicit attempts at explanation," "convenient fictions," or the like. The lesson of scientific history is unmistakable. To the hypothetical entities sketched by our theories we must venture at least provisional grants of ontological status (1963:251; emphasis in the original).

Knowledge Systems and Complementarity

Naive realism has no room for metaphysics. Mental images are but photographs of reality printed on the passive paper of the mind. Primary empirical observations present us with bits of information, and theories combine these into literal pictures of reality. No subjective interpretation is involved. Instrumentalism reduces reality to metaphysics, to the mental processes the mind uses to paint images from experiences. For critical realism, the question of abstraction is an important one, and it restores metaphysics to a central place in science. In short, it postulates a complex dialectical relationship between external realities known through experience and the mental worlds we build by means of cognitive processes.

First, we must recognize different levels of abstraction (Figure 12; cf. Kuhn 1970; Schilling 1973; and Laudin 1977). For our purposes we will differentiate four levels. At the base are our experiences of reality and the mental categories we use to sort them into a manageable number of concepts. For example, in English we speak of "trees," "rocks," "atoms," and "electricity." Moreover, we assume that these concepts correspond in some way with reality. Indeed, the concept of reality is indispensable to any understanding of languages and cultures.[5]

Above concepts are theories. These are limited, low level systems of explanation based on observation and notions of causality that seek to predict specific phenomena. They are proposed answers to the fundamental questions the scientist is asking. Often alternative theories arise that give different answers for the same set of questions. Theories themselves may be on different levels of generality, with broader theories subsuming more limited ones.

Theories, in turn, are imbedded in higher level systems of knowledge that Thomas Kuhn (1970) calls "paradigms," Larry Laudin (1977) calls "research traditions," and others refer to as "belief systems" or "cognitive systems." I will call them "knowledge systems." In the sciences, they include the "disciplines" of physics, chemistry, biology, medicine, and so on; in theology, they include systematic and biblical theology; and in everyday Western life, they include auto mechanics, electrical engineering, cooking, football, classical music, farming, and so on.

Knowledge systems are generally made up of at least three components: (1) a set of beliefs about what sorts of entities and processes make up the domain of inquiry, (2) a set of questions worth asking, and (3) a set of epistemic and methodological norms about how the domain is to be investigated, how theories are to be tested, how data are to be collected, and the like. They serve important functions in the generation of theories. They indicate what is uncontroversial "background knowledge" to scientists in that tradition, identify portions of theories that are in difficulty and need of

Levels of Mental Construction

Relationship Between Levels

Worldview
- mediates conflicts between belief systems
- provides cognitive, affective, and moral reinforcement of systems

Belief Systems
- make explicit the basic worldview assumptions
- stimulate change in worldview by mediating experiential inputs

Belief Systems
- determine legitimacy of questions
- generate conceptual problems
- perform constraining, heuristic, and justificatory role

Theories
- justify and change belief system

Theories
- select and order experiential data in the categories of the belief system
- investigate causality

Data
- force new definitions of reality on theories

World Inside
(Culture)

Worldview
- provides ontological, affective, and normative assumptions upon which the culture builds its world
- integrates belief systems into a single cultural whole

Knowledge Systems
(Research Traditions/Paradigms)
- determine domain of examination
- define questions to be asked
- provide methods for investigation
- integrate theories into a comprehensive belief system
- mediate between empirical realities and worldview

Theories
(Maps, Models)
- provide answers to questions raised by belief systems
- reduce experiential data to concepts for theoretical manipulation

Experiential Data

World Outside

Types of Problems

3rd Order:
Ultimate Problems
- ontological nature of *truth*: meaning, reality *desirable*: beauty, enjoyment, likes *righteousness*: values, morality

2rd Order:
Conceptual Problems
- internal inconsistencies in worldview or belief systems (search for internal rationality)
- external conflicts with other belief systems
- methodological problems

1st Order:
Empirical Problems
- test of fit between theories and empirical data

Figure 12

Source: Paul G. Hiebert. The missiological implications of an epistemological shift. *TSF Bulletin.* 8.5 (May–June 1985): p. 13. Used by permission. (Adapted from Laudin 1977.)

modification, establish rules for the collection of data and testing of theories, and challenge theories that violate the foundational assumptions of the tradition (Laudin 1996:83–84). Associated with any active knowledge system is a family of theories. Some of these are mutually consistent, whereas other rival theories are not. What these theories have in common is that they seek to answer the same questions, and can be tested and evaluated using the methodological norms of the research tradition.

Finally, a number of research traditions and a great deal of commonsense knowledge are loosely integrated in a larger worldview. A worldview is the most fundamental and encompassing view of reality shared by a people in a common culture. It is their mental picture of reality that makes sense of the world around them. This worldview is based on foundational assumptions about the nature of reality, the givens of life. To question them is to challenge the very foundations of life, and people resist such challenges with deep emotional reactions.[6]

How do different theories and knowledge systems such as physics, biology, and sociology relate to one another? Naive realists and idealists hold that all facts must be incorporated into a single comprehensive system of knowledge. They cannot accept two different views of the same reality. For example, most scientists will not accept the validity of theology until it is cast in scientific terms. Instrumentalists, on the other hand, hold that all systems of knowledge are simply different views of reality and do not need to be integrated. Critical realists allow for diverse views of reality, but on different premises. They claim truth for their knowledge but see theories and knowledge systems as maps or blueprints of reality. Each may give us some truth about reality, but none shows us the whole. To understand the complex nature of reality, we need a number of complementary maps or blueprints, each of which shows us truth about some aspect of the whole. For example, to understand a house, a simple photograph will not do. We need the blueprints of its wiring, plumbing, structural beams, and foundations, most of which remain unseen. Reality is too complex for our finite minds to grasp in total. We need complementary models to comprehend it.

According to the theory of complementarity (Grunbaum 1957; Austin 1967; Kaiser 1973; MacKay 1974), different views of reality can be accepted as complementary if they are embedded in a common worldview and do not contradict one another in the areas of their overlap. If there are discrepancies, these must be resolved, or one or the other of the knowledge systems must be modified or rejected. For example, if the blueprints show wiring in a wall that does not exist in the structural blueprints, one of them must be wrong.

The classic example of complementarity is found in physics. As Neils Bohr pointed out, light in some situations acts as a wave, in other situations as quanta of energy, and in still other situations as a field. The different sciences, too, are potentially complementary. Physics, chemistry, biology, psychology, sociology, and anthropology all contribute insights into the nature of reality, which none of them sees fully. Anthropologists see emic and etic analyses and diachronic and synchronic models as complementary ways of looking at reality (Headland, Pike, and Harris 1990). Complementarity holds that we need different perspectives to get a more comprehensive view of reality.[7]

Critical realism goes further. It argues that there is no qualitative difference between scientific and other knowledge systems—that these can also be complementary. Laudin argues:

> The approach taken here suggests that there is no fundamental difference in kind between scientific and other forms of intellectual inquiry. All seek to make sense of the world and of our experience. All theories, scientific and otherwise, are subject alike to empirical and conceptual constraints.... The quest for a specifically scientific form of knowledge, or for a demarcation criterion between science and nonscience, has been an unqualified failure (1996: 85–86).

As we will see, this has profound implications for the integration of theological and scientific models.

Second, to understand theories and knowledge systems, we must examine the logical processes we use in ordering our data. First level generalizations are based on empirical observations. Nature and life are crystallized in forms and structures without ever exhausting their possibilities. No two apples are exactly the same, no apple the same from one day to the next. No two experiences are identical. The ever-changing, immensely varied kaleidoscope of our experiences must be reduced to a limited number of concepts if we are to make sense out of them. It is impossible for us to have different words for each of them. Without this deceptively simple ability to group things that are not identical into sets on the basis of certain shared characteristics, we could not understand or predict events. Science is, in part, an exploration of basic structures and order that exist in the perceived world. It is here that primary verification takes place on the basis of experience as judged by reason.

Generalizations at the higher levels of knowledge involve logical processes—the mental abilities of forming abstract concepts, relating these in complex theories, and testing between competing theories. Critical realism accepts the validity of the formal algorithmic logic that is the basis for positivism and postpositivism, but it broadens the concept of rationality to include other types of reasoning. It recognizes the role of metaphors, analogies, and other tropes in shaping human thought.[8] It also recognizes different forms of logic, such as the current distinction between "concrete functional logic," "abstract propositional logic," and "pattern recognition" (Luria 1976). Laudin writes:

> On one familiar view of rationality... being rational involves meting out one's degree of belief in accordance with the probability calculus. On another view, it involves basing one's beliefs on legitimate modes of logical inference. On still another, it comes down to adopting beliefs which conduce to one's cognitive ends.

To make matters worse, "rational" functions both as a normative and a descriptive concept (1996:195).[9]

In other words, rationality is a many-splendored thing.

Differentiation between primary sense observations and higher levels of abstraction poses two types of problems in science (Laudin 1977:14–69). The first of these is empirical problems. We know that all perceptions are theory-laden, they are "tinted" by the lenses we use. Nevertheless, we treat them as if they were problems about the world. For example, we observe that heavy bodies fall toward the earth with amazing regularity. In answering "how fast do they fall?" we turn to direct observations and measurement. Laudin states:

Empirical problems are thus *first order problems*; they are substantive questions about the objects which constitute the domain of any given science. Unlike other, higher order problems,… we judge the adequacy of solutions to empirical problems by studying the objects in the domain (1977:15; italics in the original).

The second type of problem in science is conceptual problems.

[C]onceptual problems are higher order questions about the well-foundedness of the conceptual structures (e.g., theories) which have been devised to answer the first order questions (Laudin 1977:48).

There are two kinds of conceptual problems. One deals with internal inconsistencies in a theory or knowledge system. The other relates to conflicts that arise between a knowledge system and other knowledge systems held by the scientist. The aim of science is to maximize the scope of solving empirical problems while minimizing the scope of conceptual problems. In critical realism both experiential data and conceptual models are important.

Commensurability and Truth

Positivists assume that scholars in competing paradigms can comprehend and compare differences between them because they observe the same world, use the same scientific language, and abide by the same rules. Kuhn, an instrumentalist, argues that knowledge is embodied in paradigms, and that these are incommensurable. Scientists in one paradigm cannot understand or communicate with those in another because they observe different worlds, speak different languages, and follow different rules. Despite these assertions, the world is moving toward a global exchange of information that contradicts claims of incommensurability. How can we speak of "truth," and how is commensurability possible if all knowledge is indeed contextual and subjective?

Critical realists argue that paradigms can be made commensurable through the process of translation. This translation is possible for three reasons. First, people live in the same real world and share many human experiences that enable them to bridge conceptual differences. Dorothy Lee comments:

> If reality itself were not absolute, then communication of course would be impossible. My own position is that there is an absolute reality, and that communication is possible. If, then, that which the different codes refer to is ultimately the same, a careful study and analysis of a different code and the language of the culture to which it belongs should lead us to concepts which are ultimately comprehensible, when translated into our own code. It may even eventually lead us to aspects of reality from which our own code excludes us (1950:89–90).

Kenneth Pike shows how living in a common world makes it possible for people to learn new language, to compare cultures, and to translate between them with a measure of assurance that some invariant content is preserved in the course of each successful case of translation.[10] For instance, we point to a tree and say "tree," and the stranger begins to learn our language.

Second, commensurability is possible because all humans share the same kind of minds. This is not to say that there are not different systems of logic, but that people can be taught to think in new ways, just as they learn new languages. Finally, intercultural understanding is possible by means of metacultural grids. In studying two theories or cultures deeply, a person develops a translating frame that is detached from both and allows the person to translate from one to the other (Figure 13). In the scientific community, the question of what constitutes a suitable metacultural grid becomes, itself, part of the scientific dialogue (Hofstadter 1980).

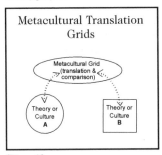

Figure 13

Commensurability helps us understand the question of truth. The concept of truth rests on our ability in a knowledge system to make a choice between competing theories and to show that one contender is superior to its rivals. The principles of comparing, testing, and evaluating theories vary from level to level of knowledge. Generally speaking, research traditions are not directly testable, both because their ontologies are too general to yield specific predictions and because they do not directly produce testable assertions about matters of fact. Their credibility rests on the theories they entail.

On the material level, positivism holds that empirical statements are true if they correspond one-to-one with reality. Instrumentalists conclude that they are creations of human minds. Critical realism recognizes that although statements are culturally shaped, they do refer in certain ways to material realities. Nevertheless, empirical statements can be made in different languages and established by independent verification. Without such reference and verification, human thoughts and communication are exercises in imagination.

On the conceptual level, positivists argued that true scientific advances are made by testing hypotheses and proving them to be true. Karl Popper (1959), however, argued that we can never prove a hypothesis true, no matter how many observations we make. One observation is enough to prove a hypothesis false. For example, we cannot prove that "all dogs have tails," even though we examine one million of them and all of them do. The next dog we examine may, in fact, have no tail, and our generalization is disproved. Popper knew, however, that we do not throw out a theory simply because there is an instance that falsifies it. If we find a tailless dog, we question whether this animal is really a dog or whether it once had a tail that was later cut off. In principle, for Popper, science is made up of theories that have at least not been proven false, even after scientists have repeatedly tried to do so.

Kuhn argues that because theories are incommensurable we cannot show one to be truer than the other. He argues that scientists normally do not test their theories by trying to prove them false. On the contrary, they assume their theories are true and work to fill in gaps of information. Nor do they throw out a theory simply because there are facts that contradict it. They reject a paradigm only when the anomalies become too great and another paradigm is offered in its place. Any paradigm is better than no paradigm, for any explanation is better than no explanation. Kuhn argues that choices between paradigms are not based on reason or hard evidence but on social and political forces in the scientific community. In other words, scientists cannot claim that their theories are true.

Critical realists accept Kuhn's idea that meaning lies not in the sum of facts but in the configuration that orders them. However, they argue that some theories can be shown to be more true than others through comparison, experimentation, and analysis. Polanyi illustrates this with a hypothetical case.

> Suppose we wake up at night to the sound of a noise as of rummaging in a neighboring unoccupied room. Is it the wind? A burglar? A rat?... We try to guess. Was that a foot-fall? That means a burglar! Convinced, we pick up courage, rise and proceed to verify our assumption (1946:22–23).

Given a few experiences, our mind automatically formulates a hypothesis—it is a thief. In trying to verify our hypothesis, two types of change can occur. First, we look for additional information that confirms our hypothesis. We go into the next room to see who is there. Second, on the basis of additional data we may have to reject our hypothesis in favor of a totally new one. We may come to the conclusion that there is no burglar, only our pet cat knocking over a lamp.

Selection between theories rests on rational as well as empirical grounds. As we have seen, both positivism and postpostivism argue that progress can be shown only if the new theory explains all the data the old one does and more. Postpositivists show that this rarely happens. They come to the conclusion that we cannot show one theory to be better than another: therefore, we cannot speak of truth or progress. Critical realists accept the validity of formal algorithmic logic such as mathematics and propositional logic, but they recognize that this constitutes only a small segment of human rationality. The fact is that most decisions, such as diagnosing an illness, buying a car, or grading a paper, are based on a careful weighting of many different variables and making an informed judgment. As Laudin points out, in science such judgments between competing theories involve evaluating a number of factors such as (1) their accounting for empirical evidence, (2) the degree to which they solve critical and stubborn problems in the field, and (3) their fertility in extending the range of what we can now explain and predict. Moreover, many theories are tentatively explored and tested before they are finally adopted over the previous explanations. Paradigm shifts are rarely sudden or total. In short, we need a much richer view of rationality—one that does not reduce it to computerlike calculations but sees it as a form of wisdom.

Although comparison and weighted judgments do not prove one paradigm to be fully true and the other totally false, they do allow us to say that one paradigm is a closer approximation of the truth than the other.[2] We need here to note the differences between "approximate" and "relative" knowledge. The latter refers to knowledge in which there is no absolute against which it can be compared. "Approximate," on the other hand, refers to knowledge related in one way or another to some reality or absolute. Approximate knowledge may not be complete or exact, but that does not make it relative or arbitrary. We may measure the table and say that it is six feet long. A careful measurement shows it to be 6.17 feet long, and more exact study shows it is 6.1735 feet long. Each of these statements is true at a certain level of exactness. They all tell us something about the actual length of the board. Approximations are tied to a reality—to a fixed given, the better the approximation, the closer it is to reality.

Approximation also has to do with scale. In positivism, every detail of knowledge must be accurate for the whole to be true. In critical realism, we recognize that there are many levels of observation (cf. Schilling 1973). We can observe a human as a whole and examine the biological, psychological, social, and spiritual processes at work in the person. Or we can examine the human on the level of cells made up of billions of organisms, each of which has a life of its own. Or we can examine the human at the atomic and subatomic level— as trillions of wave/particles separated by vast empty spaces. This may be useful for finding truth at the atomic level, but it is useless when we are driving down the freeway. On that level it is important to know the truth that "a car is approaching me in the next lane." We do not need to have exact knowledge of atoms or the inner machinery of the car to avoid hitting it. Approximation has to do with an asymptotic approach to truth. Our knowledge is always partial, and often flawed, but by careful investigation of "reality" and by reexamining our own assumptions and theories, we can gain a better understanding of truth.

Several things need to be said about the nature of truth as seen from a critical realist perspective. First, the nature and the tests for truth vary according to the nature of the statement. Referential statements are tested in terms of logical consistency, coherence, comprehensiveness of experience, and congruity with the evidence. Analogical and figurative statements are judged by the appropriateness of the similarities and likenesses they claim. Nondiscursive statements such as rituals and expressive culture point beyond ordinary language to speak of things words cannot express, such as deep feelings of awe, love, and transcendence. These can be tested only in indirect ways.

Second, we must begin our tests of truth using the best means and models we have, but in the process we can discover new tests and new models of reality. Grant Osborne notes, "[Faith] can give theories an aura of certitude, but within the community even the most established views are open to clarification and reformulation" (1991:408).

A critical realist approach to human knowledge affirms that knowledge can be true. Barbour writes:

> The critical realist takes theories to be representations of the world. He holds that valid theories are true as well as useful…. The scientist, he insists, seeks to understand not just to predict or control. Unlike the naive realist, however, the critical realist… acknowledges the incomplete and selective character of scientific theories…. No theory is an exact account of the world, but some theories agree with observations better than others because the world has an objective form of its own (1974:37).

As Harold Schilling notes, "Science actually investigates nature itself, not just its own ideas. The descriptions it develops do depict reality, but not in pictorial detail…. Science's descriptions of these are therefore to be taken as "true," though not literalistically so in detail" (1973:99).

Finally, critical realism reintroduces the importance of mystery as a part of the universe. Schilling writes:

> In the modern period it was thought that nature could in principle be described and presented completely by scientific theories that supposedly pictured reality in one-to-one correspondence between concept and physical entity…. Eventually everything would not

only be known but be told—completely, and with pre-
cision.... [Today] scientists are keenly aware that
there is probably no aspect of nature that is not inef-
fable in some degree (1973:175).

Mystery, as Schilling defines it, is not as-yet-unsolved problems—or the quantity of the unknown; rather, mystery is
what is sensed to be unknowable, incomprehensible, tran-
scendent—the quality of the unknown. "With this awareness
comes the realization that nature has also dimensions other
than those directly perceivable and conceivable by science"
(1973:31).

Hermeneutical Community

Sociologists of knowledge, such as Karl Mannheim (1952)
and Berger and Luckmann (1966), show us that science is a
social process involving a community of scientists who make
their decisions on the basis not only of hard evidence but
also of community processes. This insight undermined positivism's claims of totally objective truth discovered by the
lone scientist. Instrumentalists reduced knowledge to community beliefs and argued that this makes it totally subjective
and relative. Critical realists argue that community investigation is an essential part of the hermeneutical process of
searching for truth, and that far from undermining the
process, it is a powerful corrective against the subjective biases of individual scholars (Jarvie 1984; Fuller 1991).

Community hermeneutics involves several steps. First,
scholars in a discipline select a domain of reality to examine,
determine the critical questions for investigation, provide
categories for reflection and methods for investigation, set
the standards, define "proofs," and integrate one or more
theories into a comprehensive system of knowledge. They
also generate conceptual problems for theoretical investigation. They work in a worldview, but they seek to make
explicit its largely implicit assumptions and the biases it
introduces into their research. In short, the community provides scholars with the preunderstandings that they bring to
their analysis of questions of truth.

Second, members of the community check their research in critical interaction with one another in their search for truth. In the process, they correct one another's biases and seek for an agreement on theories based on independently verified facts and replication of the study. They test their knowledge against the history of interpretation in their discipline and the knowledge of the current scientific community. Dialogue in such a community is a non-Hegelian search for theories that explain the facts more accurately (cf. Osborne 1991:401–15). It also helps decentralize the search for truth and keeps a few from controlling knowledge for their own purposes.

Disagreements

What happens when critical realists disagree? Because they distinguish levels of knowledge, they distinguish between the nature of disagreements. Disagreements related to data are resolved primarily by repeating scientific observations or reexamining historical records. Generally speaking, these disagreements provoke less emotional confrontations and can be resolved by working together to examine the facts.

Disagreements on higher levels of theoretical abstraction are not so much over the "facts," but over the interpretation of these facts. But interpretation is the essence of theories and knowledge systems; and when interpretations are called into question, the theories and knowledge systems of which they are a part come under examination. Because theories, knowledge systems, and worldviews are configurational systems for the interpretation of facts, disagreements can lead to confrontation rather than synthesis. However, because critical realists realize that their theories are models and not photographs of reality, they are less rigidly dogmatic and are more open to examining the claims of other theories in the light of the data. Disagreements lead more to irenic debate about the truth in a spirit of humility rather than to confrontation and rejection. Moreover, changing theories is less traumatic for critical realists than for positivists, for whom the rejection of an old theory is seen as a rejection of truth itself. This does not mean that critical realists do not believe in their theories deeply. They are committed to truth and want to make certain that their theories represent it. But they realize that their knowledge is human and therefore finite and limited.

Critical Realism and Anthropology

For the most part, sociocultural anthropologists have abandoned the radical forms of cultural relativism characteristic of the mid-twentieth century as fruitless and nihilistic. They now combine two approaches to the study of human societies and cultures. The first is to seek to understand specific cultures better through "thick description" ethnographies. In these, anthropologists seek to understand other cultures deeply using emic categories and participant observation. Now, however, they also examine how their own assumptions color their interpretation of the data (cf. Geertz 1988).

Second, anthropologists compare cultures to formulate broader theories regarding societies, cultures, and human beings in general. This comparison requires the construction of etic metacultural grids.[12] Levi Strauss, A. R. Luria (1976), Mary Douglas (1970), and Victor Turner (1969) have explored the deep cognitive and social structures underlying all human systems. Morris Opler, Walter Ong, James Spradley, Oswald Werner, and G. Mark Schoefle have contributed much to our understanding of the worldviews that underlie all cultures. Darrell Forde and W. R. G. Horton (1967) have rejected a mechanistic social determinism and take knowledge systems in other cultures seriously. They help us understand human behavior in the light of the philosophical assumptions and worldviews of the people, and they reintroduce teleology as an important dimension in human thought and behavior. These studies emphasize both social and cultural differences, but also the underlying unity of all humans.

Anthropologists, however, have not found a way to move beyond phenomenology to ontological evaluations of the truthfulness and morality of different knowledge systems. In this sense, anthropologists have a long way to go in moving into a critical realist stance.

Critical Realism and Globalism

It is clear that we are moving into a new era in which all humans are becoming part of one global history. The planet has become for us a single whole. All the crucial problems have become world problems, and nothing essential can happen anywhere that does not concern us all. Schilling adds:

Contemporary man is coming to sense keenly that the world is an all-inclusive community of beings—such as the earth's matter and energy; its soil and mineral deposits, atmosphere, and waters; its plants, animals, and human beings; its things, as well as personal and social realities; its many relationships and events—all of which together constitute an integrated systemic whole rather than merely a loose collection of essentially self-sufficient, independent entities (1973:23).

Science and technology have played a key role in the development of global communication and the impact this is having on world systems of knowledge and organization. Globalization, on the other hand, has challenged the colonialism of modern science and the deconstructionism of modern philosophy, and is forcing them to see themselves as a part of the world scene, and not outside it. The implications of this for science and philosophy will be far-reaching.

Critical Realism and Christianity

How would theology and missions look in a critical realist mode, and how would they relate to the sciences? These questions must be raised if we are to get beyond the pluralism and the cultural fundamentalism of postmodernity.

Critical Realism and Theology

Theology based on a critical realism would differ in significant ways from that based on positivism or instrumentalism.

Scriptures and Theology

First, evangelical critical realists differentiate between theology and Scripture and ascribe final and full authority to the latter as the inspired, divinely superintended record of God acting in and entering human history. The Bible is divine revelation, the source and criterion against which we measure theological truth. For us it is the definitive record of the person and work of Jesus Christ.

Theology, on the other hand, is our best human understandings of the Scriptures. It is our personal and corporate confession of what we believe. To say that it is a confession is not to reflect doubt, but to affirm our strong conviction not only to understand but also to live by these truths. David Wells gives us an excellent definition of theology that fits a critical realist epistemology (1993:100ff.). He notes that theology has three elements to it: (1) a confessional element of what the church believes the Scriptures teach, (2) reflections on this confession that seek to give a comprehensive understanding of the total panorama of Scripture as well as how the church has understood the confessions in its sociocultural and historical contexts, and (3) the cultivation of a set of virtues that are firmly rooted in the first two elements. In other words, our theologies are not just models *of* divine revelation; they are also models *for* our response to that revelation. Faith is not simply cognitive affirmation of the truthfulness of a statement. Nor is it simply positive feelings toward God. It is knowledge and feelings that lead us to respond to Christ's call to follow him. As Peirce points out, "Faith is that on which we act." The goal of theologizing, therefore, is not only correct knowledge but also obedience and discipleship.

From a critical realist perspective, theology is knowledge based on symbols, models, and analogies. For instance, our understanding of an infinite God can only be in our finite categories and experiences. We think of God as reasoning and as acting like a person, even though we know that Isaiah is right when he says (55:8), "'For my thoughts are not your thoughts, neither are your ways my ways,' says the Lord."

Does the model nature of human knowledge lead us to theological relativism? In critical realism the answer is a strong no. As we have seen, in any model there must be correspondence between the model and that with which it is compared—between a map and the reality it maps. Although no model provides a complete picture of reality, and although it simplifies or omits nonessential information so that the human mind can grasp certain essentials, it must be accurate on those essentials if it is to serve as a true and useful map.

Theology in Context

As critical realists, our theologies are rooted in the Scriptures. They are also influenced by our sense percepts and the ways our minds work, by the language we use and our hermeneutical processes, by our personal interests, by the culture and community in which we participate, and by the historical context in which we live. We may "see through a glass darkly," not because of the limits of divine revelation but because of the limits of our human knowledge. On the other hand, given the triadic nature of symbols, our knowledge is related to reality; therefore, "we do see." During the colonial era, scholars, missionaries, and pastors emphasized the biblical text. They had little awareness of the ways culture and historical contexts shaped the way they and their audiences understood the text, particularly in cross-cultural settings. During the anticolonial era they focused on the contexts and were in danger of losing sight of the text. In a global perspective, we turn our attention again to the texts but seek to understand them in the contexts in which they occur as well as in the many human contexts in which the words are communicated.

The contextual nature of theology raises a difficult question. Committed Christians in different historical and cultural contexts develop theologies that differ in the categories they use, the questions they answer, and the assumptions they make. We must, therefore, speak first of theologies, for each theology is a human understanding of divine revelation in a particular historical and cultural context. Thus we speak of the theology of Calvin, or of Luther, or of Evangelicalism. This does not deny Theology—truth as God knows it. Rather, it recognizes that all human theologies are partial and culturally biased, and that the truth in the Scriptures is greater than our understanding of it. There is room, therefore, for spiritual maturation and growth in our theologies, but this means we must constantly test our theologies against Scripture and be willing to change them when we gain new understandings of it. Divine revelation and historical realities do not change, but our understandings of them do.

Does this pluralism not undermine the unity of the gospel? In an attempt to develop a single New Testament theology, some writers have denied portions of the Scriptures. For example, Marcion in the early church appealed to Paul and Luke against the writings of the earliest apostles, whom he accused of being caught up in Judaism. In the end he defined a canon consistent with this Pauline stance (Goppelt 1971:107). Similarly, Luther began with Paul and the Epistle to the Romans, and relegated the Epistles of James and Hebrews to a level of secondary importance. Many post-Enlightenment theologians, in search of a unified systematic theology in the New Testament, have sought to fit scriptural passages into their theological molds by forced interpretations or elimination of certain texts.

Paul himself, however, recognized theological diversity in the early church and saw this variety as an expression of the freedom of faith, and of the many forms that the Spirit's work can take (1 Cor. 12:4–6; Eph. 4:1–7). As L. Goppelt points out:

> In Paul's view the *multiplicity of theologies does not fundamentally place the unity of the church in doubt;* for no congregation prescribes for itself a standard theology and no New Testament writing intends to offer such a theology. There are neither Paul nor Johannine congregations! (1971:121; emphasis in the original).

Confronted by the fact that some claimed to follow the teachings of Apollos and others the teachings of Paul or Peter, Paul neither tries to show that all three in fact agree theologically nor affirms his claims against the others. Rather, he affirms the central doctrines of the gospel that define true Christianity—namely, the historicity of Christ's incarnate birth, death, resurrection, and ascension (1 Corinthians 15; 1 Tim. 2:5–16, 2 Tim. 2:8), the coming of the Holy Spirit to guide believers into the truth (1 Cor. 2:12–13), and the immanent return of Christ—as these are revealed to us in Scripture (2 Tim. 3:16). For him, the unity of the church lay in a common and total allegiance to the person of the crucified and risen Christ. To deny this is not simply another theological point of view; it is another gospel—a false doctrine, a heresy (Gal. 1:6–11).[13] Neither Paul nor the early church allowed for theological relativism. They defined truth in terms of the biblical canon and the church creeds, and in obedience to the gospel that leads to transformed lives (2 Tim. 2:14). Bosch (1991:56–178) shows how Matthew, Luke, and Paul cast different lights on the person of Jesus and the mission of the church without contradicting one another.

How do we resolve the tension between theological absolutes and theological pluralism—between Theology and theologies? The answer lies, in part, in developing a theology of how to do theology—in other words, a metatheology (Hiebert 1988).

Hermeneutical Communities

A metatheology must recognize the fact that different persons in different cultures understand the Scriptures differently. It must also enable them to work together toward a common understanding of the truth of Scripture. A critical realist approach to theology must begin with Scripture. It is God's revelation to us, not human reflections about God (although it contains these). It is God revealing himself to us from outside our human predicaments. Theologizing must be led by the Holy Spirit, who instructs us in the truth. We need also to recognize that the same Holy Spirit at work in us is also at work in the lives of believers in other contexts. Theologizing must also affirm the priesthood of all believers and recognizes that they must and will take the universal message of the Bible and apply it to their own lives and settings. It must recognize that different people ask different questions when they read the Scriptures, and that their cultural and historical frameworks will color their interpretations. Finally, theologizing must be done in community. It is ultimately the task not of individuals but of the church. C. Norman Kraus notes:

> Thus the Scripture can find its proper meaning as witness only within a *community of interpretation*. Principles of interpretation are important, but secondary. There needs to be an authentic correspondence between gospel announced and a "new order" embodied in community for Scripture to play its proper role as a part of the original witness. The authentic community is the hermeneutical community. It determines the actual enculturated meaning of Scriptures (1979:71).

Does not community hermeneutics lead us to instrumentalism and a consequent theological relativism? No. Historical realities remain the same in all times and cultures, and although our interpretation of history introduces a subjective dimension, the facts of history force on us a large measure of objectivity. In Scripture we see clearly the great events of time—creation, fall and redemption, and Christ's life, death, and resurrection. Second, community hermeneutics guards us against the privatization of faith and from our personal misinterpretations of Scripture. Just as others see our sins more clearly than we see our (personal and cultural) own, so they see our theological biases and errors more clearly that we do. Similarly, the cultural biases of local churches must be checked by the international community of believers in all cultures and ages. Furthermore, we must remember that God is continually at work in his church, shaping and reshaping it into his likeness.

Does this approach undermine the role of leadership and specialized studies in the hermeneutical community? A hermeneutical community is not a democracy in which decisions are reached by majority vote. It is a community seeking truth and as such draws heavily on the insights of specialists who master different areas of study relevant to the field of analysis. Just as in a medical procedure there are doctors with different specializations, nurses, laboratory technicians, and informed patients, so in theology we need specialists in biblical exegesis, specialists in systematic and biblical theology, homileticians, and lay church members acting as a single community.

Disagreements

Faced with disagreements, positivists attack one another as false, instrumentalists smile and go their own ways, idealists split, and critical realists go back and search the Scriptures to test their different points of view.

Problems arise, however, when critical realists disagree with Christian colleagues with other epistemic foundations. Critical realists can accept theological disagreements without calling the Christian commitment of others into question, so long as they are willing to accept the authority of Scriptures as divine revelation. Critical realists are willing to continue the dialogue in their common search of Scripture to resolve disputes. If this fails, they maintain relationships despite disagreements because they know that one or both parties may have misunderstood the biblical texts, and because they are called to love everyone. Positivists, on the other hand, are compelled by their epistemic position to take a confrontational stance. They can tolerate no theological differences or accept theologies as different interpretations of Scripture. Failing in their attempts to convert critical realists, the former must accuse them of heresy and reject further communication and fellowship. The fact is that many disagreements in theology have less to do with the contents of theology than with its epistemic nature. Until this is resolved, there can be little meaningful theological deliberation.

Theology and Science

How does the integration of theology and science look from a critical realist perspective? First, we recognize that there can be no true integration between a science based on one epistemology and a theology based on another. A science based on realism and a theology based on idealism simply talk past each other. Second, we would reject the old view

that science is based on *facts* and theology is based on *faith*.
This view is so deeply ingrained in Western thought that
even Christians and theologians make the distinction.
Critical realists argue that science is not a distinct way of
knowing, nor is it logically prior to other forms of inquiry or
superior to them as a way of knowing. In other words, theology and science *are not different ways of knowing*. Both
seek to make sense of the world and of our experiences
(Jarvie 1984:19–63; Laudin 1996:85). Both begin with belief
in their underlying premises and draw on historical experiences to help them understand the order and meaning in
reality.[14] Both assume a real world characterized by an order
that is continuous over time. Both assume the ability of
human reason to understand the world, at least in part. They
are different knowledge systems because they ask different
questions, use different methods of analysis, and draw certain types of conclusions. This has profound implications for
us as Christians, for it means that we must proclaim theological truth as public truth—true for everyone, not just
those who believe it (Newbigin 1991).

From a critical realist perspective, science, theology, philosophy, and other knowledge systems are not antagonists
but are potentially complementary. We need different knowledge systems to examine the world around us. We need theology to understand the cosmic history of all creation. We
need the sciences to help us understand the material and
social world around us.

However, juxtaposing different knowledge systems does
not assure us of integration. We can deal with different knowledge systems piecemeal and end with a "stratigraphic
approach" to reality. For integration to take place, the knowledge systems must truly be complementary. This requires
first that they both be embedded in the same worldview. Just
as it is impossible to integrate a theology based on idealism
with a science based on realism, we cannot integrate theology with a science that denies God's existence. We must begin
with a biblical worldview and then develop our theology and
our science within this overarching framework of givens.[15]

Second, complementarity requires that we deal with problems that arise between knowledge systems. When contradictions appear, we need to examine again our theology and our science against the data and seek to resolve the disagreements.

There is a second type of complementarity that we need to explore—that between synchronic and diachronic systems of knowledge. The former seek to understand the structures of reality, how these operate and the functions they serve. For example, a synchronic analysis of a human would include an analysis of the body, its various structures such as bones, muscles, and nerves; its various systems such as blood circulation, digestion, and reproduction; and the way it thinks and moves. This approach looks also at the effects of various diseases on the body. Diachronic systems of knowledge, on the other hand, look at the history of specific realities. A diachronic analysis of a person would examine her or his life story. It would look at various events in the lives of one or more individuals and the forces at play and their responses.

Complementary Knowledge Systems		
	Diachronic Models	Synchronic Models
Theology	Biblical theology Historical theology	Systematic theology
Science	Historical sciences	Natural and social sciences

Figure 14

This distinction helps us understand the complementary nature of the sciences. Most, such as physics, chemistry, biology, psychology, sociology, and anthropology, are predominantly interested in synchronic analysis. Scientists examine the structure and operation of matter, life, persons, groups, and cultures. History is predominantly interested in diachronic questions. The distinction also helps us to understand theology. Systematic theology is synchronic in that it examines the unchanging nature of God and the fundamental structures of creation. Biblical theology is diachronic; it looks at God's acts and revelation in specific cultural and historical settings, and the experiences of God's people down through history. We use both in seeking to understand

Scripture. As we study the history of events recorded in the Bible, we automatically formulate universals in our minds. When we focus on theological universals, specific historical scenes come to mind. One or the other may be in focus and the other in the background, but both are needed to understand truth revealed to us in the Bible. Taken together, science and theology, diachronic and synchronic paradigms, provide us with a better understanding of reality (Figure 14).

Critical Realism and Missions

What are the consequences for the critical realist with a global perspective for missions? First, globalization requires a reevaluation of mission history. During the colonial era, Christian writers presented Western missionaries in a totally positive light. Later, anticolonial writers painted them as servants of colonialism and destroyers of cultures. In recent years, historians such as Lamin Sanneh have begun to reinterpret mission history from a global perspective. They see both the good and the bad in the modern mission movement, and recognize that, despite its weaknesses, the movement did plant the church throughout the world. Globalization, however, not only changes how we view missions but also how we do it (Figure 15).

Evangelism, Conversion, and Discipleship

How do epistemic positions influence our attitudes toward evangelism and discipleship? Because idealists and naive realists claim to know objective truth, they tend to see evangelism as the proclamation of theological verities. They often attack other religions to discredit them with the hopes that their followers will then turn to Christ. But this rarely works; attacks and arguments rarely win people. Non-Christians see this polemical stance as arrogant and accuse the missionaries of being more interested in proving correct doctrine than in listening to them as humans.

Critical realists hold to objective truth but recognize that it is understood by humans in their contexts. There is, therefore, an element of faith and personal commitment in the

Epistemological Shifts in Western Thought

	Modernity	Postmodernity	Globalism
Epistemology:	Positivism	Instrumentalism	Critical Realism
• nature of knowledge:	- photograph	- Rorschach, mental	- maps, blueprints, models
• goal:	- truth	- pragmatism and problem solving	- Truth/truth and problem solving
• nature of truth:	- absolute	- perspectival, relative	- absolute/perspectival, approximate
• knowledge:	- objective	- subjective	- objective/subject
• unity:	- GUT	- deconstructionist and incommensurable, Kuhnian paradigms	- complementary interrelated models, common human experience
• view of reality:	- reductionist	- pluralistic, fragmented	- integrative
• perspective:	- in culture A	- in culture B	- metacultural perspective
Anthroplogy:	Evolution	Functionalism	Postfunctional
• culture and humanity:	- unity of humanity and civilization	- diversity of humanity and cultures	- unity/diversity of humanity and cultures
• viewpoint:	- etic	- emic	- etic/emic
• truth:	- absolute	- relative	- absolute/relative
• communication:	- sender oriented	- receptor oriented	- correspondence oriented
• theory:	- one comprehensive theory	- particularistic theories	- integration of several comprehensive theories
Theology:	Theology	Theologies	Metatheology
• nature:	- systematic, comprehensive	- deconstructionist, pluralist	- metatheology leading to community-based theology
• focus:	- text (theology)	- context (social sciences)	- text in context (theology and social sciences)
• hermeneutics:	- literal	- interpretive	- double horizon
Missions:	Colonial	Anticolonial	Global
• other religions:	- displacement	- dialogue for consensus	- dialogue to find truth
• translation:	- formal	- dynamic equivalence	- double translation
• symbols:	- form=meaning	- form/meaning	- form, meaning, reality
• contextualization:	- noncontextualization	- uncritical contextualization	- critical contextualizaiton
• need:	- real need	- felt need	- real and felt needs
• message:	- West to East	- discovery from within	- from above to all cultures
• missionary:	- outsider, proclaimer, "God's lawyer"	- insider, fellow seeker, learner	- incarnational, witness, sharer of Good News
• attitude:	- confrontational	- nonconfrontational	- hard love

Figure 15

knowledge of truth. This subjective appropriation of objective truth has several consequences. First, critical realists have deep convictions about the truth and bear testimony to them. Mission to non-Christians begins in witness—in affirming, as the church has affirmed in all its great confessions, "I believe..." This is an act of confession in which we not only attest to the truth and our submission to it but also to our participation in the church. It is also a public proclamation of the gospel to the world that carries the power of confessing faith calling others to that faith (cf. Acts 26:16; 2 Tim. 1:12). E. Stanley Jones captures this approach to evangelism when he writes, "When I was called to the ministry, I had a vague notion that I was to be God's lawyer; I was to argue his case for him and put it up brilliantly." After describing his failure in this approach, Jones continues:

> This was the beginning of my ministry, I thought—a tragic failure. As I was about to leave a pulpit a Voice seemed to say to me, "Haven't I done anything for you?" "Yes," I replied, "You have done everything for me." "Well," answered the Voice, "Couldn't you tell that?" "Yes, I suppose I could," I eagerly replied. So... [I] said, "Friends, I see I cannot preach, but I love Jesus Christ. You know what my life was in this community— that of a wild reckless young man—and you know what it now is." ...I got the lesson never to be forgotten: in my ministry I was to be, not God's lawyer, but his witness. That would mean that there would have to be living communion with Christ so that there would always be something to pass on. Since that day I have tried to witness before high and low what Christ has been to an unworthy life (1925:141).[16]

Second, critical realists respect people of other beliefs as thinking adults and show respect for their convictions. They are not interested in winning an argument but in winning the lost to Christ.

Critical realist Christians take conversion seriously. For them, this is not simply a mental acceptance of a set of theological truths. It is a change in a person's central allegiance and a personal commitment to follow Christ in life and in death. It is both a point and a process. Justification and sanctification are inseparable elements of the same transformation. This means leading people to faith in Christ and discipling them into Christian maturity. This does not mean a total rejection of everything from a person's or community's cultural past. Truths and practices from the old can be incorporated in the new if they can be given new meanings compatible with the biblical paradigm. This is why building theological reflection into the life of a young church is so crucial. Evangelism without solid theological reflection produces a weak and syncretistic church. Theological reflection without evangelism creates a Christian club.

Finally, a global perspective requires a recognition of both felt and real needs. Colonial missions focused on the ultimate need for salvation; anticolonial missions looked to the felt needs of food, liberation, justice, and self-esteem. Today we realize that we must bring a whole gospel—one not divided between the Greek dualism of eternal salvation and human needs. We may need to start with felt needs, but we must move to the ultimate human needs of salvation, reconciliation, justice, and peace, both here and in eternity.

Multiplex Translation

A global perspective requires a new theory of translation. During the colonial era, Bible translation was formal. It was assumed that if one translated the forms, the meanings would follow. Further analysis showed that this assumption was not true. People reinterpret what they hear in terms of their own cultures and worldviews. This concern led to dynamic translations that sought to preserve meanings by changing forms. Carried too far, they reduced meanings to subjective perceptions in the heads of people.

The solution offered by a triadic view of signs is a multiplex translation in which we seek to preserve both meanings and forms. We now know that we cannot totally divorce

forms from meanings because the relationship between them
is different for different kinds of signs (cf. Nida and Reyburn
1981). In some, like names in the West, the linkage is loose,
and we are more free to change the forms in translation.
Others, such as analogies, parables, and allegories, are based
on inherent similarities between the sign and the reality to
which it refers. Still others refer to historical facts where
form and meaning are intrinsically linked to each other and
cannot be separated in translation. For example, Jesus was
born in Bethlehem, and this is true for all people in all languages and cultures. In translations, we seek to preserve the
linkage of form, concept, and reality as it is found in the original text. This is done, in part, by preserving the literary
genre. Poetry needs to be seen as poetry, parable as parable,
and history as history. At times this is done by keeping the
original forms and adding commentary notes to make their
meaning clear. For example, "shekels" are not translated into
"dollars"; rather, a footnote gives the approximate value of a
shekel in dollars for readers who have no idea of what a
shekel is worth. At other times, it is done by using appropriate analogies. For example, a noted Korean artist painted a
series of pictures on the life of Christ in which Christ is
depicted as a Korean teacher. In it Christ is wearing the
black hat that was the traditional Korean symbol of a
teacher. The houses and the clothes are also in Korean style.
If the artist were to claim that his pictures represent historical facts, his drawing would be false. But he was trying to
depict the deep truth, namely, that Christ identified himself
with all humanity, including the Koreans, in his life and
death. The symbolism here is not literal but allegorical. The
awareness of the role of analogy in translation has given rise
in recent years to an interest in what is called "redemptive
analogies" (cf. Richardson 1984).

This translatability of the gospel has made it global.
Lamin Sanneh points out:

 Translatability is the source of the success of
  Christianity across cultures. The religion is the willing

adoption of any culture that would receive it, equally at home in all languages and cultures, and among all races and conditions of people (1989:51).

It is also the source of the bewildering variety of Christian expressions.

Modern semiotics has also made us aware of the importance of rituals as nondiscursive enactments that speak of realities that cannot be reduced to mere words, and that change social and spiritual realities.[17] Modern missions must become much more aware of rituals, importance in contextualizing the gospel in the lives of people in different cultures.

Critical Contextualization

Our epistemic stance has implications for how we view contextualization. The response of positivist missionaries to other cultures has often been one of radical displacement. Consequently, to become Christian, the people had to become Western. In reaction, anticolonial advocates called for contextualization, assuming that all cultures are good and that all forms of Christianity are syncretistic to some degree. Global missionaries take a critical approach to contextualization. For them, cultures are not morally neutral entities, and cultural change cannot be a matter of ethical indifference. They see good in all cultures, because culture is created by humans and humans are created in the image of God. But they also see evil in all cultures and societies, for human sin is not only individual but also corporate and systemic. Critical contextualization is the ongoing response of the church that sees the gospel as outside culture. It comes as the message of salvation, not from West to East, but from God to people in all cultures. For them to hear and believe, the gospel must be communicated in ways that they understand and value but that do not distort the gospel.[18] As William Dyrness (1990) points out, our concern to communicate the gospel in culturally sensitive ways must be guided by two commitments: effective communication and fidelity to biblical truth.

There are several steps in the process of critical contextualization. First, the church and its members must recognize
the need to deal biblically with all areas of life. Discerning the
areas that need to be critiqued is one of the important functions of the church. Second, the church must study the traditional cultural ways associated with the question at hand.
In doing so, the church must seek to understand these ways
deeply, as the non-Christians see them. Third, the church
must study the Bible with regard to the question at hand. This
is a crucial step, for if the people do not clearly understand
and accept the biblical teachings, they will be unable to deal
with their cultural past. Finally, congregations must evaluate
their own past customs in the light of their new biblical
understandings, and create new ways that express their
Christian faith authentically in their culture.

A congregation may respond to old beliefs and practices in
several ways. Many of these will be kept, for these are not
unbiblical. Some will be rejected as contrary to the gospel.
Some the members will reinterpret, giving them explicit
Christian meanings. The members will also adopt foreign
ways, such as baptism and the Lord's Supper, to express their
unity with the church worldwide, and they will also create new
rituals that express the gospel in fresh ways in their culture.

Toward a Global Theology and Church

How do critical realists deal with the theological pluralism that
has appeared as churches are planted in different cultures? As
we have seen, in Paul's view theological pluralism within limits does not place the unity of the true church in doubt.

First, critical realist missionaries recognize that committed
Christians in different cultures will interpret the Scriptures
within their specific contexts (Figure 16). Consequently, different theologies are bound to emerge because different cultures ask different questions, and because they view reality
in different ways. For example, Indian Christians ask what
should be the church's response to the caste system and
whether they can use Indian words such as *deva, Brahman,*

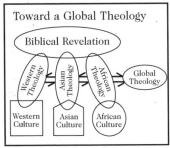

Figure 16

avatar, and *moksha* for God, incarnation, and salvation. These terms carry Hindu connotations. Introducing English words, however, makes the gospel unintelligible to the people. In many tribal societies, the questions facing young Christians are what to do with polygamy, with the spirits and powers surrounding them, and with witchcraft. Latin American theologians must struggle with the biblical response to oppression of peasants and the poor. But missionaries must also check for their own cultural biases. As Robert Linder and Richard Pierard point out (1978), Western Christianity is in danger of becoming a civil religion justifying Western national and cultural systems.

Second, because critical realists affirm truth in theology, they must deal with these differences. They cannot accept mutually contradictory theological positions. Different theologies may be complementary because they address different needs and situations, and use different methods of biblical analysis, but where contradictions do emerge, they must be resolved by further examining the Scriptures.

Third, the global church must become an international hermeneutical community in which Christian leaders from around the world become partners in hermeneutics—seeking to understand Scripture under the guidance of the Holy Spirit, to help one another in dealing with the problems they face in their particular contexts, and to check one another's cultural biases. Out of this process there can emerge a global theology that is increasingly freed from the influences of specific human contexts. This is beginning to happen as theologians from different parts of the world gather to address various issues such as theology of ancestor veneration (Ro and Eshenaur 1984), and of caste (Ro 1985).

This view of the gospel and of the church affects the way we do missions. Our first task is to translate the Bible and to train Christians to read and interpret the Scriptures in their own cultural context. Although we are deeply persuaded about our own theological understandings, we recognize that the Holy Spirit is at work in the lives of young believers, guiding them in their understanding of the truth. We must also recognize that the greatest contribution we can make is to build churches that are communities in which the Scriptures are read, interpreted, and obeyed. Finally, we must work toward a global church in which Christians living under the authority of Scripture become a missionary community, calling people to faith and challenging the evils around them.

Christianity and Non-Christian Religions

How does a critical realist epistemology affect our attitudes toward non-Christian religions? As we have seen, positivists and idealists are compelled by their epistemologies to reject other religions as totally false, and with them the beliefs and customs associated with them. Conversion requires a total rejection of old ways. The result is a combative approach to other religions. Instrumentalists, on the other hand, see all religions as culture bound and as serving useful functions in their respective societies. Missionaries, therefore, should seek to help others be better people in their own religions, learn from them, and look for areas of dialogue and consensus.

How do we respond to other religions from a critical realist epistemic stance? First, we affirm our common humanity with all people. Critical realism does not see modern knowledge systems as a totally new way of knowing reality. Consequently, we must respect and love all people as fully human like us, and we must study and take their religions seriously. To affirm our common humanity is to recognize that all humans live in God's creation and have the ability with their God-given senses and minds to comprehend the world in part. It is also to recognize commensurability between humans and cultures that enable us to relate to them no matter how different our cultures are, and to share with them the gospel we ourselves have received from missionaries from other times and cultures. In affirming the oneness of humanity, we do not deny the great difficulty of understanding people in other cultures. Far too often we claim to know what others are thinking and feeling, when, in fact, we are totally wrong. The more we study cultural differences, the more we realize how difficult true cross-cultural communication really is, and how important it is to study the people's culture and religion to communicate and build relationships of love and trust with them.

It is here that interreligious dialogue of one kind is indispensable to Christian mission to people of other religions. The Lausanne Covenant notes, "Our Christian presence in the world is indispensable to evangelism, and so is that kind of dialogue whose purpose is to listen sensitively in order to understand (point four)." Here dialogue helps us to build understanding and trust with non-Christians, to find bridges of communication with them, and to help us discriminate between truth and error in their beliefs. It can also challenge us to reexamine our own understandings of and commitment to our biblical faith.

Dialogue can also help us define moral codes that can serve as the basis for government in modern nations. Today people of different faiths must cooperate politically on national and international levels to build peace and justice. In these interreligious consultations we must not compromise our ultimate allegiance to the Kingdom of God and its righteousness, nor blur the distinctions between religions. What we cannot do in dialogue is to join in interreligious rituals in which we "share in one another's spirituality," or compromise our conviction that Christ is the only way to God and that all other gods are false gods.

Critical realist Christians reject religious relativism and affirm the uniqueness of Christ and the authority of Scripture, and they do so not in arrogance because they are in some way superior to other people, but in love, seeking to extend the Good News of salvation to all who suffer under the tyranny of sin.

Where does this leave us as Christians in missions? God has mightily used the modern mission movement to plant churches around the world, but it is clear that we cannot and do not want to go back to a positivist, colonial approach to missions. Nor can we take a postmodern approach that sees all religions as human searches for God and rejects Christian mission as calling people to faith in Jesus Christ. We need to follow Paul's lead when he writes, "But speaking the truth in love, we must grow up in every way into him who is the head, into Christ" (Eph. 4:15, NRSV). We need the hard love that compels us to speak the truth, and the hard truth that points us to Christ who so loved the world that he gave his life for it. The great missionary A. G. Hogg wrote out of his experience as a missionary: "Merely look at Jesus and you behold a Man. But meet him face to face in the inwardness of comradeship and obedience, of faltering need and kingly succor, and you know yourself to be meeting the very Person, the very Self of God. I do not explain this; I simply testify" (1922:65–66). In mission, our central task is not to communicate a message but to introduce people to that person, Jesus Christ.

Notes

Chapter 1:
The Epistemological Foundations of Positivism

1. I write from the perspective of a committed evangelical Anabaptist theology. This will be evident particularly in my approach to theological and missiological applications of a critical realist epistemological position. I write also as a practicing anthropologist and missiologist seeking to make the Good News of God's salvation known among all peoples.

2. "Realism" has a variety of meanings, depending on use and context. Following Harold Netland's lead, I will distinguish between the ontological distinctions of "realism" and "nonrealism." Realism affirms that there is some reality that has ontological existence apart from consciousness. Nonrealism denies this and holds that reality is the product of individual or collective acts of consciousness. Further, I will examine different epistemological positions in realism such as naive realism and critical realism. Too often these two sets of issues are conflated, resulting in unnecessary confusion.

It is important to note that there are different realist ontologies. One of the most influential is what some call "scientism," a form of positivism that, as Netland points out, "holds the view that the physical universe is all that there is;

that all 'knowledge' must be 'verifiable' or demonstrated in some conclusive sense; [and] that the 'hard sciences' provide the paradigm for all true knowledge." As Christians, we reject scientism, but we affirm realism—the fact of a real world created by God but distinct from him, and a real history of events in that world.

3. The term "positivism" was used first by Henri, comte de Saint-Simon, to designate the scientific method and its extension to philosophy. It was developed by Auguste Comte in his *Cours de Philosophie Positive*, 6 vols. (1830–42) and his *Catechisme Positiviste* (1852). For Comte, "positive philosophy" meant real, certain, relational philosophy, and positivism was a philosophical system founded on positive facts and observable phenomena. He believed that positive sciences and the scientific method determined positivist doctrine.

Logical Positivism, as a specific school of thought in philosophy, emerged in the 1930s in Germany. For an excellent discussion of it see John Passmore's *A Hundred Years of Philosophy* (1966). In its broader sense, positivism is widely used in the literature to refer to the epistemological foundations for modern science. Ian Barbour (1974) refers to the epistemology as "naive realism," but this label is somewhat pejorative in its connotations. Others refer to it as logical empiricism and objectivism. I will use "positivism" to refer to the broad epistemology underlying many of the modern sciences, as Laudin, Leplin, and many other contemporary writers do.

4. Steven Fuller (1991:5) notes: "Before Kant philosophers typically understood the nature of knowledge and the nature of reality as two sides of the same coin.... The point of the Kantian critique—at least as it was taken by Kant's successors—was to detach the question about knowledge from the question about reality... [making it] conceptually possible in the nineteenth century to practice epistemology as something distinct from metaphysics."

5. Fuller (1991:177) points out that this dissociation took place in the scientific community of Victorian England under the leadership of John Tyndall.

6. E. A. Burtt (1954) and E. J. Dijksterhuis (1986) examine the metaphysical foundations of modern science.

7. Immanuel Wallerstein notes that in the late eighteenth century a "divorce" occurred between science and philosophy that led to the emergence of C. P. Snow's "two cultures." Before that people did not make a strong distinction between them. In the nineteenth century science was defined as "the empirical, the search for truth through research, as opposed to what philosophers did, which was to speculate or make deductions in some way. It was a continuation of the break between philosophy and theology; this was taking it one step further, toward a thoroughly secularized knowledge system" (1996:1). Allan Bloom (1987) points out that this divorce led after the Enlightenment to a shift in terminology from "morals," which imply a sense of absolutes, to "values," which are socially based and relative.

8. Although scientists did not pass moral judgment on what they observed, they did require scientists to be honest in reporting their findings. The ethics of science have been much debated, particularly in its use for destructive purposes such as war.

9. One consequence of this was to take education out of the homes and guilds and put it in schools controlled by scientifically educated teachers. Universities became the cathedrals of higher education.

10. Paul Gossman (1996) traces the modern discussion on different systems of rationality.

11. This was written shortly before the discoveries of radioactivity, X rays, quantum mechanics, and Einstein's theory of general relativity! Some scientists now estimate we may know 5 percent of what there is to know about the physical world.

12. At this point, modern science broke with Greek philosophers such as Plato, who believed in inevitable degeneration and decay—inevitable because it was prescribed by the nature of the universe. The Cartesian mechanical theory of the world and invariable law, carried to a logical conclusion, excluded the doctrine of Providence and replaced it

with Progress (Bury 1960:8–20, 69–126). This belief in progress was articulated by Comte in his "law of Three Stages," which later became the basis for an evolutionary approach to the study of history.

13. Positivism is intrinsically reductionist in nature. It cannot allow different and complementary ways of looking at things to coexist side by side without seeking to reduce one to the other.

14. Historically, between 1750 and 1850, there were hundreds of names for research inquiry. Between 1850 and 1914 these were reduced to six major names and a couple of minor ones (Wallenstein 1996:2).

15. As Clifford Geertz points out, one value of this stratigraphic approach is that it guarantees the established academic disciples their independence, provides jobs for different specialists, and guarantees them a living.

16. An example of this is A. H. Maslow's hierarchy of needs (1962), which has had devastating effects on modern mission practices. As Geertz points out (1979), physical needs are not the deepest of human needs. Moreover, if we seek to meet all the lower needs before we turn to spiritual ones, we will never get to the latter.

17. Two images of the Other were dominant in Europe during the Middle Ages. The first of these was that of "monsters." North Europeans had stories of gargantuan humanoids who were embodiments of evil. After the coming of Christianity, these monsters were seen as the "descendants of Cain." The second image was that of the Muslims, who were seen as Infidels—humans who had rejected God.

18. Rudolf Bultmann notes: "...the intervention of supernatural powers in the course of events; and the conception of miracles... we call mythological because it is different from the conception of the world which has been formed by science... and which has been accepted by all modern men" (1958:15).

19. We will see in Chapter 2 that the term "culture" was not used in the present sense until about 1930; the battle between the two words was a fierce one in anthropology.

20. This emphasis on cognitive knowledge as the sine qua non for ministry has led to an explosion of educational institutions around the world and the pursuit of academic degrees.

21. Einstein forged his theories of special relativity (1905) and general relativity (1916) as a positivist, but he underwent a philosophical conversion when he was forty-one (1920), when he became deeply committed to critical realism. His later battle with quantum theory was fought more over epistemological foundations than over determinism, as is often portrayed (Fine 1984:91–92).

Chapter 2: The Epistemological
Challenges of Instrumentalism and Idealism

1. Laudin (1996:4) includes Kuhn, Feyerabend, the later Wittgenstein, the later Quine, and the later Goodman among those he calls "postpositivists." For a good discussion of instrumentalism, also known as constructionism, see Leplin 1984.

2. We see Wittgenstein's shift in his later years to an instrumentalist view of language in *Philosophical Investigations* (1953).

3. For a brief discussion of de Saussure's theoretical views, see Culler 1977.

4. Laudin (1996) argues that instrumentalism is kin to positivism because it sees algorithmic logic as essential in determining truth.

5. To say a theory is a "useful fiction" does not mean it is false. It is not like a "fictitious name," which is a kind of deliberate deception. Nor is it like a "legal fiction" (e.g., that a corporation is a person), which a court treats as if it were true, though it is known to be false. A "useful fiction" is a mental construct used instrumentally for particular purposes but is not assumed to be either true or false. Often we can show that one theory helps us to deal with the problems we face in life better than the others, so we adopt it.

6. Interestingly enough, the term "pragmatism" was first coined by Charles Peirce, who defined it as a form of critical realism. When his students, William James and John Dewey,

hijacked the movement and made it a form of instrumentalism, Peirce dissociated himself from pragmatism and tried to start another movement named "pragmaticism" (1958:180–223).

7. We must differentiate between critical idealism based on ontological skepticism (we do not know for sure if there is a mind-independent reality "out there," and we have no access to it if it is there) and absolute idealism, which denies the existence of external realities—a position of ontological nonrealism.

8. In 1968 Thomas Oden wrote of postmodernity but used it to refer to what comes after modernity and what is now widely called "postmodernity"—that is, deconstructionism. He argues that what are now called "postmodernists" are, in fact, ultramodernists. We will follow the more generally accepted definition of postmodernity as used by authors such as Laudin (1996), Harvey (1990), and Hassan (1985), and represented by such writers as M. Foucault, J. Derrida, and J. Lyotard.

9. For good analyses of the underlying social cultural systems of early modernity, see Berger et al. (1974), Ellul (1964), Harvey (1990). For a discussion of the conflict between modernity and postmodernity, see Rosenau (1992), particularly pp. 167–84.

10. For a good analysis of deconstructionism, see Osborne 1991: 380–86.

11. Most "true believers," defined in the social sciences as those committed to certain beliefs irrespective of the evidence for or against them, would probably be idealists.

12. We see this in Advaita Hinduism, which holds that external realities are maya or illusion, and that behind all phenomena is a single-force field. The same monism is seen in many branches of the New Age movement in the West.

13. For an analysis of the theories of formal and dynamic equivalence translations, see Nida 1964.

14. In two reviews of thirteen books published from 1985 to 1989 dealing with Christianity and non-Christian religions (Clooney 1989; Knitter 1989), only one, that by S. Mark Heim (1984), takes a strong stand on the uniqueness of Christ as the only way to salvation. For an excellent recent book defending the uniqueness of Christ in salvation, see Netland 1991.

15. This new discipline first gained public attention at the "World's Parliament of Religions" held in Chicago in 1893. A contemporary example is the "World's Parliament of Religions" held in Chicago in 1995.

16. Sanneh (1993) notes that the incarnational nature of the gospel makes it translatable into other languages and cultures without losing its truth and power. On the other hand, fundamentalist Muslims forbid the translation of the Qur'an lest its exact meanings be lost. To be a true Muslim, therefore, one must learn Arabic, live in an Islamic state, and practice the Muslim culture.

17. We should note that a rejection of instrumentalism as the epistemological foundation for the fundamental beliefs of a people for whatever reason does not preclude scientists from using models that they know to be useful fictions. All scientists recognize that many times it is useful to develop models for which no claims of truthfulness are made. The question is not whether all mental models depict reality, but whether any, particularly those most fundamental to our beliefs, do. As we will see, the critical realist makes truth claims chiefly for the fundamental models that are central to his or her paradigm.

18. In anthropology the attack against relativism has gone so far that Clifford Geerts, in the distinguished lecture of the American Anthropological Association (1984), titled his speech "Anti-Anti-Relativism." He argues that relativism was a good corrective to the parochialism of Western thought. Today most anthropologists are not calling for a return to claims of Western intellectual superiority or to a unified theory that downplays cultural differences. Rather, they look to a multi-perspectivalism (what we will look at later as "complementarity") that argues that people in different cultures can, in some important ways, understand and evaluate one another.

Chapter 3:
Critical Realism—A Way Ahead

1. One of the founders of this form of realism was Charles Peirce (1955; 1958), an American mathematician,

linguist, and philosopher at the turn of the century. More recent advocates of critical realism, sometimes known as "scientific realism," are Ian Barbour (1974), Jarrett Leplin (1984), and Larry Laudin (1996).

2. All cultures differentiate the colors (1) red, (2) black, (3) white, and (4)yellow-green-blue. Cultures that have five words for basic colors either split yellow from green-blue, or blue from green-yellow. All cultures with six or more colors have the basic set of black, white, red, yellow, green, and blue. The wavelengths of light and the physiological processes of the brain determine cross-culturally valid boundaries for color categories.

3. It is analogical in the technical sense of correspondence, likeness, or agreement between the relations of things to one another, a partial similarity between two things.

4. For a good discussion of changes in paradigms or "plausibility structures," see Berger and Luckmann (1966:147–63). We need to be careful in speaking of "paradigm shifts" because the term itself tends to draw us into an instrumentalist view of knowledge.

5. In defining "reality" it is important that we avoid the positivist notion that it is what science reveals to be the case. Rather, we must begin with what people in different cultures believe to be "real," including those in the culture of science, and then we must examine these in the light of Scripture and "reality testing," processes we will examine later.

6. "Critical realism challenges the Cartesian scepticisim of positivism and affirms that all knowledge systems must begin with beliefs, not doubt. These beliefs have to do with the basic nature of things, the fundamental assumptions people make about reality. Over time these assumptions may be challenged by experience and reason" (Peirce 1955, 228–50).

7. Instrumentalists tell of five blind men feeling an elephant and coming to different conclusions as evidence that all knowledge is subjective. If these men shared their findings with one another and realized that each felt a part of the whole, they could come closer to the truth.

8. Paul Friedrich (1991) lists five ways in which the mind orders data: imagistic, modal, contiguity-based, analogical,

and formal or algorithmic. He points out that none of these is a subtype of any other; none is logically derivable from some yet more comprehensive supertrope or "unique beginner," and they are not related to each other in a highly organized or rule-governing way. Rather, they are theoretically open-ended and interact in complex ways. Further study is needed to explore the logic used in American law in which deductions are based on the analysis of a great many different cases.

9. Laudin gives a modest definition of rational action and belief: "A rational agent is one who has various prior beliefs about the world. His rationality consists in his engaging in a process of ratiocination in order to ascertain what course of action his goals and prior beliefs commit him to. To adopt a belief rationally, the agent must be able to specify reasons, relative to his goals and background knowledge, for adopting that belief rather than its negation" (195).

10. See Pike 1993. The preservation of meaning in communication has led to an extensive discussion of the nature of the "meaning" in "texts"—books, inscriptions, and other symbolically coded items, that are neither "knower" or "known" but "knowable." For a discussion of this, see Fuller 1991:51–61.

11. Recent theories of successive approximations of truth are rooted in Popper's original conceptualization of "verisimilitude." For a discussion of some of these theories, see Fuller 1991:65–98. Laudin, however, questions the validity to the concept of approximation (1996).

12. In a sense, anthropology is a science seeking to create metacultural grids that enable us to understand, translate, and compare different cultures. The central question in comparative anthropology is which metacultural grid best serves these purposes.

13. Paul frequently appealed to Scripture and to the confessional statements of the early church in supporting his theological positions. Examples of this are 2 Cor. 6:16–18; Phil. 2:5–11; 1 Tim. 2:5–6, 3:16; and 2 Tim. 2:8, 11–13, 19.

14. We often overlook the fact that science is based on the observation of thousands of events, each a historical moment. Theology, too, is based on historical events as these are recorded in the Scriptures.

15. Some argue that there is no biblical worldview—that the gospel can be encoded adequately in all worldviews. But then the gospel is only surface information, not a whole new way of looking at reality. The Old Testament is the record of God choosing a people to be his representatives demonstrating and proclaiming the Kingdom of God to all nations. Only a select few responded in obedience. The Old Testament is also the record of God preparing a worldview adequate for us to understand the coming of Christ. Certainly, Abraham was saved with his imperfect worldview, for a correct worldview is not essential to the conversion of an individual. But God began to teach Abraham that he is not only El as the world knew El but El Shaddai, El Elyon, El Olam, and so on. In this he was changing Abraham's worldview from a pagan understanding of God to a biblical understanding of him. Later God revealed himself more fully to Moses (the tabernacle, sacrifices, and Exodus) and to the prophets. By the time Christ came, the people of Israel had a worldview of God adequate (not perfect) to understand his coming as the Messiah. Similarly, the Old Testament shows a growing understanding of other key worldview categories such as creation, time, human, fall, sin, sacrifice, salvation, church, and eternity.

16. It was on this basis that Jones later established his effective Round Table method for witnessing to Hindus and Muslims (1925).

17. For example, when ministers say, "I pronounce you husband and wife," they not only announce the wedding—they create it by transforming the bride and groom into a married couple. Legally they are now husband and wife in society. Spiritually, from a sacramental point of view, they are joined together as one in the sight of God. A minute before they say their vows, either can call off the wedding. After they say it, the couple must go through a divorce or annulment to undo the marriage.

18. For further discussion of critical contextualization, see Hiebert 1985:171–92 and 1994:75–92.

References Cited

Alexander, W. L. 1888. *A System of Biblical Theology.* Edinburgh: T. & T. Clark.

Ashley, Richard, and R. B. J. Walker. 1990. Speaking the Language of Exile: Dissident Thought in International Studies. *International Studies Quarterly* 34:259–68.

Augustine. 1976. *The Confessions of Saint Augustine.* Franklin Center, Pa.: The Franklin Library.

Austin, J. L. 1962. *How to Do Things with Words.* Oxford: Clarendon Press.

Austin, William. 1967. Complementarity and Theological Paradox. *Zygon* 2:365–81.

Barbour, Ian G. 1974. *Myths, Models and Paradigms: A Comparative Study in Science and Religion.* New York: Harper & Row.

Berger, Peter L. 1970. *The Sacred Canopy.* Garden City: Doubleday & Co.

Berger, Peter L., and Thomas Luckmann. 1966. *The Social Construction of Reality: A Treatise in the Sociology of Knowledge.* Garden City: Doubleday & Co.

Berger, Peter, et al. 1974. *The Homeless Mind: Modernization and Consciousness.* New York: Vintage Books.

Berlin, Brent, and Paul Kay. 1969. *Basic Color Terms: Their Universality and Evolution.* Berkeley: University of California Press.

Bloom, Allan. 1987. *The Closing of the American Mind.* New York: Simon & Schuster.

Bosch, David J. 1991. *Transforming Mission: Paradigm Shifts in Theology of Mission.* Maryknoll: Orbis Books.

Boyd, Richard N. 1984. The Current Status of Scientific Realism. In *Scientific Realism*, edited by Jarrett Leplin. Berkeley: University of California Press.

Brown, James. 1955. *Subject and Object in Modern Theology.* New York: Macmillan.

Bultmann, Rudolf. 1958. *Jesus Christ and Mythology.* New York: Scribner's.

Burtt, E. A. 1954. *The Metaphysical Foundations of Modern Science.* Garden City: Doubleday Anchor Books.

Bury, J. B. 1960. *The Idea of Progress: An Inquiry Into Its Growth and Origin.* New York: Dover Publications.

Butterfield, Herbert. 1950. *Christianity and History.* New York: Scribner's.

Carnap, Rudolf. 1958. *Introduction to Symbolic Logic and Its Applications.* Trans. William Meyer and John Wilkinson. New York: Dover Publications.

Clooney, Francis X. 1989. Christianity and World Religions: Religion, Reason and Pluralism. *Religious Studies Review* 15:198–204.

Culler, Jonathan. 1977. *Ferdinand de Saussure.* Harmondsworth, Eng.: Penguin Books.

Dijksterhuis, E. J. 1986 (original 1950). *The Mechanization of the World Picture: Pythagoras to Newton.* Princeton: Princeton University Press. Eng. trans. 1961.

Douglas, Mary. 1970. *Natural Symbols.* New York: Random House.

Dyrness, William. 1990. *Learning About Theology from the Third World.* Grand Rapids: Zondervan.

Ellul, Jacques. 1964. *The Technological Society.* New York: Random House.

Farquhar, J. N. 1971 (original 1913). *The Crown of Hinduism.* New Delhi: Oriental Books.

Feyerabend, Paul. 1970. Problems of Empiricism: Part II. In *Nature and Function of Scientific Theories.* Pittsburgh: University of Pittsburgh Press, 275–353.

Fine, Arthur. 1984. The Natural Ontological Attitude. In *Scientific Realism,* edited by Jarrett Leplin. Berkely: University of California Press, 83–107.

Finger, Thomas N. 1985. *Christian Theology: An Eschatological Approach.* Vol. 1. Scottdale, Pa.: Herald Press.

Firth, Raymond W. 1973. *Symbols, Public and Private.* Ithaca: Cornell University Press.

Friedrich, Paul. 1991. Polytropy. In *Beyond Metaphors: The Theory of Tropes in Anthropology.* Stanford: Stanford University Press, 17–55.

Fuller, Steven. 1991. *Social Epistemology.* Bloomington: Indiana University Press.

Geertz, Clifford. 1965. The Impact of the Concept of Culture on the Concept of Man. In *New Views of the Nature of Man,* edited by John R. Platt. Chicago: University of Chicago Press, 93–118.

Gellner, Ernest. 1992. *Postmodernism, Reason and Religion.* London: Routledge & Kegan Paul.

Gergen, K. 1986. Correspondence Versus Autonomy in the Understanding of Human Action. In *Metatheory in Social Science,* edited by Donald W. Fiske and Richard A. Shweder. Chicago: University of Chicago Press.

Giddens, Anthony. 1990. *The Consequences of Modernity.* Stanford: Stanford University Press.

Gödel, Kurt. 1992. *On Formally Undecidable Propositions of Principia Mathematica and Related Systems.* New York: Dover Publictions.

Goppelt, L. 1971. Die Pluralitat der Theologien im Neuen Testament und die Einheit Besevangeliums as Okumenisches Problem. In *Evangelium und Einheit,* edited by V. Vajta. Göttingen: Vandenhoeck & Ruprecht.

Gossman, Paul. 1996. Causal Thinking in the Prayer Practices of Traditional and Christian Spiritual Leaders of the Kankanaey (Philippines). Ph.D. diss., Trinity Evangelical Divinity Schools, Deerfield, Ill.

Graff, Gerald. 1979. *Literature Against Itself.* Chicago: University of Chicago Press.

———. 1979. Religion as a Cultural System. In *Reader in Comparative Religion,* edited by W. A. Lessa and E. Z.

Vogt. New York: Harper & Row. 4th ed.

———. 1984. Anti-Anti-Relativism. *American Anthropologist* 86:(2):263–78.

———. 1988. *Works and Lives: The Anthropologist as Author.* Stanford: Stanford University Press.

Griffiths, R. B. 1980. Is Theology a Science? *Journal of American Scientific Affiliation* September, 169–73.

Grunbaum, A. 1957. Complementarity in Quantum Physics and Its Philosophical Generalizations. *Journal of Philosophy* 54:713–27.

Hall, Edward J. 1977. *Beyond Culture.* Garden City: Anchor Books.

Harris, Marvin. 1980. *Cultural Materialism: The Struggle for a Science of Culture.* New York: Vintage Books.

Harvey, David. 1990. *The Condition of Postmodernity: An Enquiry into the Origins of Culture Change.* Cambridge, Mass.: Blackwell Publishers.

Hassan, I. 1985. The Culture of Postmodernism. *Theory, Culture and Society* 2:119–32.

Headland, Thomas N., Kenneth L. Pike, and Marvin Harris. 1990. *Emics and Etics: The Insider/Outsider Debate.* Newbury Park, Calif.: Sage Publications.

Heim, S. Mark. 1985. *Is Christ the Only Way? Christian Faith in a Pluralistic World.* Valley Forge, Pa.: Judson Press.

Heisenberg, Werner. 1962. *Physics and Philosophy: The Revolution in Modern Science.* New York: Harper & Row.

Herskovits, Melville. 1972. *Cultural Relativism.* F. Herskovits, ed. New York: Random House.

Hick, John. 1987. *The Myth of Christian Uniqueness: Toward a Pluralistic Theology of Religions.* Maryknoll: Orbis Books.

Hiebert, Paul G. 1985. *Anthropological Insights for Missionaries.* Grand Rapids: Baker Book House.

———. 1988. Metatheology: The Step Beyond Contextualization. In *Retrospect and Prospect: A Missiology for 2001,* edited by Hans Kasdorf. Bad Liebenzell, West Germany: Liebenzeller Missions Verlag.

———. 1989. Form and Meaning in the Contextualization of the Gospel. In *The Word Among Us,* edited by Dean S.

Gilliland. Dallas: Word Publishing.

——. 1994. *Anthropological Reflections on Missiological Issues*. Grand Rapids: Baker Book House.

Hofstadter, D. R. 1980. *Gödel, Escher, Bach*. New York: Vintage Books.

Hogg, A. G. 1922. *Redemption from This World, or the Supernatural in Christianity*. Edinburgh: T. & T. Clark.

Hollis, M., and S. Lukes. 1982. *Rationality and Relativism*. Cambridge, Mass.: MIT Press.

Horton, W. R. G. 1967. African Traditional Thought and Western Science. *Africa* 37:50–71, 155-87.

Hunn, Eugene. 1982. Utilitarian Factor in Folk Biological Classification. *American Anthropologist* 94:830–47.

James, William. 1946 (original 1907). *Pragmatism: A New Name for Some Old Ways of Thinking*. New York: Longmans, Green & Co.

Jarvie, I. C. 1984. *Rationality and Relativism: In Search of a Philosophy and History of Anthropology*. London: Routledge & Kegan Paul.

Jones, E. Stanley 1925. *The Christ of the Indian Road*. New York: Vintage Books.

——. 1928. *Christ at the Round Table*. New York: Abingdon Press.

Kaiser, Christopher. 1973. Christology and Complementarity. *Religious Studies* 12:37–48.

Knitter, Paul. 1985. *No Other Name? A Critical Survey of Christian Attitudes Toward the World Religions*. Maryknoll: Orbis Books.

——. 1989. Making Sense of the Many. *Religious Studies Review* 15:204–09.

Korbzybski, A. 1994. *Science and Sanity: An Introduction to Non-Aristotelian Systems and General Semantics*. Englewood, NJ: Institute of General Semantics.

Kraus, C. Norman. 1979. *The Authentic Witness: Credibility and Authority*. Grand Rapids: Eerdmans.

Kuhn, Thomas S. 1970. *The Structure of Scientific Revolutions*. Chicago: University of Chicago Press. 2d ed.

Laudin, Larry. 1977. *Progress and its Problems: Towards a Theory of Scientific Growth*. Berkeley: University of

California Press.

——. 1996. *Beyond Positivism and Relativism: Theory Method and Evidence.* Boulder: Westview Press.

Lee, Dorothy. 1950. Lineal and Nonlineal Codifications of Reality. *Psychosomatic Medicine* 12:89–97.

Leplin, Jarrett, ed. 1984. *Scientific Realism.* Berkeley: University of California Press.

Levy-Bruhl, Lucian. 1985 (original 1926). *How Natives Think.* Princeton: Princeton University Press.

Linder, Robert D., and Richard V. Pierard. 1978. *Twilight of the Saints: Biblical Christianity and Civil Religion in America.* Downers Grove, Ill.: InterVarsity Press.

Luria, A. R. 1976. *Cognitive Development: Its Cultural and Social Foundations.* Cambridge, Mass.: Harvard University Press.

Lyotard, Jean-François. 1984. *The Postmodern Condition: A Report on Knowledge.* Trans. Geoff Bennington and Brian Massouri. Minneapolis: University of Minnesota Press.

Macintosh, H. R. 1964. *Types of Modern Theology: Schleiermacher to Barth.* London: Collins.

MacKay, D. M. 1974. Complementarity in Scientific and Theological Thinking. *Zygon* 9:225–44.

Mannheim, Karl. 1952. *Essays on the Sociology of Knowledge.* London: Routledge & Kegan Paul.

Maslow, A. H. 1962. *Toward a Psychology of Being.* New York: Van Nostrand.

McGrane, Bernard. 1989. *Beyond Anthropology: Society and the Other.* New York: Columbia University Press.

Miller, Jay. 1982. Matters of the (thoughtful) Heart: Focality or Overlap. *Journal of Anthropological Research* 38: 274–87.

Murphy, Nancy, and James McClendon, Jr. 1989. Distinguishing Modern and Postmodern Theologies. *Modern Theology* 5:191–214.

Nash, Leonard. 1963. *The Nature of Natural Science.* London: Little, Brown & Co.

Netland, Harold. 1991. *Dissonant Voices: Religious Pluralism and the Question of Truth.* Grand Rapids: Eerdmans.

——. 1996. Personal correspondence.

Newbigin, Lesslie. 1989. *The Gospel in a Pluralist Society.*

London: SPCK.

———. 1991. *Truth to Tell: The Gospel as Public Truth*. Grand Rapids: Eerdmans.

Nida, Eugene. 1964. *Towards a Science of Translation*. The Hague: E. J. Brill.

Nida, Eugene, and William Reyburn. 1981. *Meaning Across Culture: A Study on Bible Translating*. Maryknoll: Orbis Books.

Nott, Kathleen. 1971. *Philosophy and Human Nature*. New York: Dell Publishing.

Oden, Thomas. 1992. *Agenda for Theology: After Modernity What?* Grand Rapids: Zondervan.

Osborne, Grant R. 1991. *The Hermeneutical Spiral*. Downers Grove, Ill.: InterVarsity Press.

———. 1996. Personal correspondence.

Oxtoby, Willard. 1968. *Religionswissenschaft* Revisited. In *Religions in Antiquity: Essays in Memory of Erwin Ramsdell Goodenough,* edited by Jacob Neusner. Leiden: E. J. Brill.

Panikkar, Raimundo. 1981. *The Unknown Christ of Hinduism: Towards an Ecumenical Christophany*. Maryknoll: Orbis Books.

Passmore, John. 1966. *A Hundred Years of Philosophy*. London: Duckworth.

Peirce, Charles S. 1955 (original 1940). *Philosophical Writings of Peirce,* edited by Justus Buchler. New York: Dover Publications.

———. 1958. *Charles S. Peirce: Selected Writings*. New York: Dover Publications.

Pike, Kenneth L. 1993. *Talk, Thought and Thing: The Emic Road Toward Conscious Knowledge*. Dallas: Summer Institute of Linguistics.

Pobee, John. 1982. Political Theology in the African Context. *African Theological Journal* 11:168–72.

Polanyi, Michael. 1946. *Science, Faith and Society*. Chicago: University of Chicago Press.

———. 1957. *Personal Knowledge*. Chicago: University of Chicago Press.

Popper, Karl. 1959. *The Logic of Scientific Discovery*. New

York: Basic Books.

———. 1983. *Realism and the Aim of Science,* edited by W. W. Bartley. London: Routledge & Kegan Paul.

Quine, Willard. 1969. Two Dogmas of Empiricism. In *Problems in the Philosophy of Language,* edited by T. Olshewsky. New York: Holt, Rinehart & Winston.

Richardson, Don. 1984. *Eternity in Their Hearts.* Ventura, Calif.: Regal Books.

Ro, Bong Rin, ed. 1985. *Christian Alternatives to Ancestor Practices.* Taichung, Taiwan: Asia Theological Association.

Ro, Bong Rin, and Ruth Eshenaur, eds. 1984. *The Bible and Theology in Asian Contexts.* Taichung, Taiwan: Asia Theological Association.

Rosenau, Pauline M. 1992. *Post-Modernism and the Social Sciences: Insights, Inroads and Intrusions.* Princeton: Princeton University Press.

Russell, Bertrand. 1918–1919. Philosophy of Logical Atomism. *Monist* 28–29.

Sanneh, Lamin. 1989. *Translating the Message: The Missionary Impact on Culture.* Maryknoll: Orbis Books.

———. 1993. *Encountering the West: Christianity and the Global Cultural Process.* Maryknoll: Orbis Books.

Schilling, Harold. 1973. *The New Consciousness in Science and Religion.* London: SCM Press.

Schwartz, Joel. 1990. Antihumanism in the Humanities. *The Public Interest* 99:29–44.

Shenk, Wilbert.1980. The Changing Role of the Missionary: From "Civilization to Contextualization." In *Missions, Evangelism and Church Growth*, edited by C. Norman Kraus. Scottdale, Pa.: Herald Press, 33-58.

Smith, Houston. 1982. *Beyond the Post-Modern Mind.* New York: Crossroad.

Strong, A. H. 1972 (original 1912). *Systematic Theology.* Philadelphia: Griffith and Rowland.

Sukenick, Ronald. 1976. Upward and Juanwards: The Possible Dream. In *Seeing Castaneda,* edited by Daniel Noel. New York: Putnam.

Taber, Charles R. 1991. *The World Is Too Much With Us: "Culture" in Modern Protestant Missions.* Macon: Mercer

University Press.

Torrance, T. F. 1978. *Theological Science.* Oxford: Oxford University Press.

Tracy, David. 1979. *Blessed Rage for Order: The New Pluralism in Theology.* New York: Seabury Press.

Turner, Victor W. 1969. *The Ritual Process: Structure and Antistructure.* Ithaca: Cornell University Press.

Wallerstein, Immanuel. 1996. Open the Social Sciences. *Items.* New York: Social Science Research Council.

Weber, Max. 1958 (original 1904–1905). *The Protestant Ethic and the Spirit of Capitalism.* Trans. Talcott Parsons. New York: Scribner's.

Wells, David. 1993. *No Place for Truth.* Grand Rapids: Eerdmans.

Wittgenstein, Ludwig. 1953. *Philosophical Investigations.* Oxford: Oxford University Press.